GARRY KNOX BENNETT

CALL ME CHAIRMAKER

GARRY KNOX BENNETT

CALL ME CHAIRMAKER

BELLEVUE ARTS MUSEUM

Published in conjunction with the exhibition *Garry Knox Bennett: Call Me Chairmaker* organized by Bellevue Arts Museum, July 6 – November 26, 2006.

All works are courtesy of the artist unless otherwise noted.
All images © M. Lee Fatherree unless otherwise noted.
All dimensions are given in inches, height precedes width precedes depth.

Copyright © 2006 by Bellevue Arts Museum. All rights reserved. No part of this book may be reproduced or transmitted in any form or by any means, electronic or mechanical, including photocopy, recording, or any other information storage and retrieval system without permission in writing from Bellevue Arts Museum.

Executive Director and Chief Curator Michael W. Monroe
Exhibition Curator Stefano Catalani
Editing by Kathleen Moles
Design by Phil Kovacevich

Front Cover: *GR Series # 6: "Wing Chair,"* 2003, lacewood, lacquer, polished aluminum, 41 3/4" x 29 1/4" x 17"

Back Cover: (top) *Thonet*, 2004, chair, fiberglass, enamel paint, hand-caned seat, 34 1/2" x 25" x 17"
(middle) *GR Series #5: "Chas Rietveld,"* 2003, enameled wood, paint, nickel-plated brass, 54 1/2" x 15" x 17 1/8"
(bottom) *Modernized Nakashima*, 2004, mahogany, polished brass, 36 1/4" x 18 1/2" x 24"

Frontispiece: *Prototype Series #2: "Red Chair,"* 2004, painted wood, aluminum, upholstered canvas, 30 3/4" x 20" x 27"

ISBN 0-942342-11-9

Published by Bellevue Arts Museum, Bellevue, Washington.

Printed and bound in Canada by Friesens Book Division.

Bellevue Arts Museum illuminates and enriches the human spirit through art, craft and design.

Bellevue Arts Museum
510 Bellevue Way
Bellevue WA 98004
Phone (425) 519 – 0770
Fax (425) 6370-01799
E-mail info@bellevueart.org

The exhibition *Garry Knox Bennett: Call Me Chairmaker* has been organized by Bellevue Arts Museum and is partially funded by:

TABLE OF CONTENTS

7   DIRECTOR'S FOREWORD

9   GARRY KNOX BENNETT: FURNITURE SCULPTOR
      MATTHEW KANGAS

17   GARRY KNOX BENNETT GETS IT IN THE END
      GLENN ADAMSON

21   ONE ARTWORK OR TWO: *NAIL CABINET* AND ITS NO-FRILLS SHIPPING CASE
      ARTHUR C. DANTO

23   PLATES

77   GARRY KNOWS BEST: A CONVERSATION WITH THE ARTIST
      STEFANO CATALANI

88   EXHIBITION HISTORY

91   BIBLIOGRAPHY

93   CHECKLIST OF THE EXHIBITION

95   ACKNOWLEDGMENTS

96   BELLEVUE ARTS MUSEUM TRUSTEES

DIRECTOR'S FOREWORD

Garry Knox Bennett: Call Me Chairmaker succinctly demonstrates Bellevue Arts Museum's mission of illuminating and enriching the human spirit through art, craft, and design. While commonly thought of as three separate disciplines, Bennett's physically and visually interactive chairs fully converge these fields into a seamless whole.

Bennett's oeuvre can best be characterized by a free-spirited attitude combined with irreverence and abandonment of established, conventional rules for the formal principles of the canons of craftsmanship. Despite his boisterous bravado and professed disdain for validated practices, Bennett fails to mask his finely tuned and well-developed sense of art, design, and craftsmanship. Underlying his seemingly spontaneous and direct designs lies a master of calculation. It looks so easy. It is not.

On behalf of Bellevue Arts Museum I want to express my deep appreciation to Garry and Sylvia. It has been a pleasure working with them on various projects over a number of years. As Curator-in-Charge of the Smithsonian American Art Museum's Renwick Gallery, I had the pleasure of acquiring for the Nation's Collection one of his most significant pieces of furniture — *Boston Kneehole*, 1989. In 1996, while I was president of Peter Joseph Gallery in New York City, Garry created a series of 100 lamps featuring disparate materials with some of the most original designs I had ever seen. Now, ten years later, the pleasure of working together returns with this series of chair explorations, his most ambitious to date.

While every exhibition is the outcome of several individuals, each pursuing his or her disciplines, I especially want to thank Stefano Catalani, the Museum's Curator, for a provocative and insightful interview with Garry Knox Bennett and for his leadership in bringing the exhibition and publication to their full fruition. To our authors — Glenn Adamson, Arthur C. Danto, and Matthew Kangas — each of whom brought their considerable scholarship combined with passion to their respective essays, I thank you.

There are numerous tasks that are the responsibility of the staff: development officer Karen Porterfield, registrar Gena Schwam, financial officer Janet Ellinger, education director Lori Osseward, external affairs director Renate Raymond, exhibition preparator Donna Keyser, executive assistant Marguerite Stanley and intern Rachel May Evans. To each, I am deeply indebted and thankful for their remarkable talents, loyalty, and steadfastness.

To Bellevue Arts Museum's Board of Trustees, Docents, Guild Members, and Volunteers, I want to express my deep appreciation for their enthusiasm and support of the Museum's mission.

We are most grateful to Microsoft for their support of the exhibition and publication.

Michael W. Monroe
Director and Chief Curator

Chinese Platform Chair #5: Late Oaktown Dynasty; 1934– ____., 2005, lacquered wood, PVC, 23K & 24K gold leaf, velvet upholstery, 39" x 22" x 26"

GARRY KNOX BENNETT

FURNITURE SCULPTOR

MATTHEW KANGAS

The distinguished American furniture artist Garry Knox Bennett (b. 1934) has capped the triumph of his 2001 American Craft Museum retrospective with a new body of work that confirms his already substantial achievement and raises fascinating new critical questions about his status within the contemporary art world. Several new series in the current exhibition extend ideas Bennett began or explored before 2001. They expand and deepen the Oakland, California resident's relation to the past as well as the present, not to mention implying several directions for his future course. At 71, Bennett is in no way resting on his laurels.

His status within the American craft world is secure. One journal even called him "king of the studio furniture universe"[1] and he has been hailed and lauded repeatedly on both coasts, exhibiting regularly in New York since 1977, with important solo exhibitions there at Peter Joseph Gallery in 1993, 1994, and 1996, as well as successive showings at Leo Kaplan Modern in 1999, 2001, 2002, and 2003.

However, perhaps because of a variety of interviews in which he proclaims himself a humble maker rather than artist, critical commentary has sometimes been at a loss to situate Bennett. True, no less than Pulitzer Prize-winning art critic Arthur C. Danto annexed Bennett onto one strain within 20th-century art history: the "altered readymade," first seen with Marcel Duchamp's *Fountain* (1917), a porcelain urinal inverted and signed by the artist's alter ego, R. Mutt. Danto's discussion of Bennett's *Nail Cabinet* (1979; p. 20) in the retrospective publication, *Made in Oakland: The Furniture of Garry Knox Bennett*, is extensive, setting the work in an august lineage that also includes, among other subversive artworks, Robert Rauschenberg's *Erased de Kooning Drawing* (1953).[2] The only problem with Danto's analogy, his shoehorning of Bennett into a particular branch of contemporary art genealogy is that, except for a show of lamps, little of Bennett's work has been found or "readymade." There may be a rejection of industrial perfection and uniformity or crafty preciousness, but Bennett's hammering of a nail into a pristine padouk wood surface in *Nail Cabinet* has far

Wiggle Wright, 2004, mahogany, upholstered mohair, 23K gold leaf, 36" x 22" x 16"

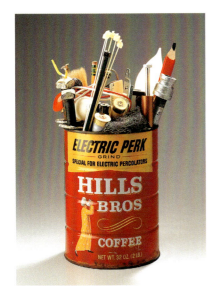

Hills Brothers, 1996
Can, miscellaneous found objects, lamp parts, 11 1/2" x 6 1/2"

Charles Rennie Mackintosh (1868–1928)
Chair for the Hill House, 1903
55 1/8 x 16 x 13 3/8"
Vitra Design Museum

fewer significant ramifications than Danto grants. In fact, Danto's essay presents a basic misunderstanding of Bennett's overall oeuvre. Humor, yes; categorical critique of the world of manufactured objects, never. Constructed, handmade objects, yes; altered readymade, rarely until now (as we shall see below).

The other approach to Bennett has to do with an opposite attempt, wrenching him out of the art world and repositioning him in the murky depths of American decorative arts history. Cautious, careful, and conscientious, Edward S. Cooke, Jr.'s approach in the museum publication cemented Bennett's links to American handmade furniture history. Context and precedent are all for Cooke, as for most art historians. He places Bennett in the stew of Funk art, at least—the San Francisco Bay Area art movement begun with a group show in Berkeley, California, in 1967 that became so influential with painters and ceramic sculptors. Cooke's tracing of Bennett is meticulous and detailed but sheds little light on the aesthetic meaning of the objects.

Curvy, colorful, erotic, and even on occasion scatological, at the time, Funk art liberated hundreds of artists seeking alternatives to strict East Coast requirements for sculpture such as modernist "truth to materials," not to mention increasing prohibitions on representational imagery, color, and embellishment. For our purposes, examining Bennett's recent work, it might be helpful to remember Funk art but to also bear in mind the two carefully argued analyses of Danto and Cooke and seek out a third approach that has been largely overlooked or denied: Garry Knox Bennett is a sculptor.

Free to disregard the artist's statements to the contrary, the viewer can now encounter Bennett's art in all its chromatic, three-dimensional, ornamented glory. To sit or not to sit, that is not the question (my dear Arthur), but whether to gaze again, walk around, and delight in the multiple layers of meaning, color, process, and volume. Seen this way, the viewer may have a fresher, quicker access to these works.

Just as numerous turned-wood sculptors may claim previously unaccorded links to early modern wood sculptors like Barbara Hepworth, Jean Arp and Henry Moore,[3] so Bennett's art might make more sense by reviewing its sculptural aspects akin to early modern furniture designers and their apex of stark forms, banished ornament, scant color, and a horror of decorated surfaces. Bennett's liberation as a sculptor involves as much an embrace as a rejection of early 20th-century design movements and masters.

As we shall see, his quotations of the chairs of Duncan Phyfe (1768?–1854); William Morris (1834–1896); Frank Lloyd Wright (1867–1959); Charles Rennie Mackintosh (1868–1928); Josef Hoffmann (1870–1956); Gerrit Rietveld (1888–1964); George Nakashima (1905–1990); Charles Eames (1907–1978); and Philippe Starck (b. 1949), create a pantheon of design giants that Bennett literally cuts down to size in the work in this exhibition. Studio strategies of fragmentation, reconstruction, and the violation of plain surfaces by color, pattern, marking, and other various drastic re-fashionings of identifiable design icons comprise the artist's simultaneous

Gebrüder Thonet
Chair No. 18, 1875–76
35 5/8 x 16 1/2 x 20 1/2"
Vitra Design Museum

claim of ownership to those predecessors and his compulsive need to betray, correct, and "improve" their signature chair designs. By stressing the handmade appearance and by making each of his works absolutely unique, Bennett is also rescuing or redeeming the cold and heartless industrial look to the earlier works.

Since Bennett's new chairs are not a substitution for other kinds of his art, as one could say of Donald Judd's (1928–1994) chairs, tables, and desks, Bennett's chairs are his sculptural statements. They are not all really usable, or are in the way that Judd's and Scott Burton's (1939–1989) are: bold sculptural statements that take the form of chair as subject matter. If Judd could make sculpture into chairs, why can't Bennett make chairs into sculpture? To stand rather than to sit seems a more apposite question of their function.

Garry Knox Bennett, like Wendell Castle (b. 1932), Albert Paley (b. 1944), and Dale Chihuly (b. 1941), is a crossover artist from the craft world to the art world. In this sense, his art is closer to not only Castle, Paley, and Chihuly, but also to other artists embracing eccentric form, colored and decorated surfaces, and furniture subject matter, like Lucas Samaras (b. 1936), Ken Price (b. 1935), and Richard Shaw (b. 1941). Favoring polychrome, not monochrome, these artists successfully kept open sculpture's option during the repressive minimalist and post-minimalist periods.

Bennett's sly references to the modern architecture and design giants link him to their austere aesthetic tangentially. His treatments of their design motifs become facets of his own sculptural practice, not its central meaning. The multi-sided, painted, gilded, and even upholstered object is a way of sidestepping the reductive abstraction of most modern sculpture, a strain that culminated in large-scale abstract sculpture. Bennett restores the intimacy of scale in his contemporary sculpture, using fine woods, metals, and other materials to shore up the compelling powers of the handmade object without recourse to jewelry or the tiny pedestal-size of Price's cups, let alone the gigantism of Ronald Bladen (1918–1988) and Alexander Liberman (1912–1999).

Bennett's retrospective in New York (and at the Oakland Museum of California) elicited a variety of responses from the art and craft worlds. Danto's canonization of Bennett into the Warholian family tree of Brillo boxes and Duchamp's urinals was one view. Another critic, Jonathan Binzen, took the opposite approach. Lamenting that "this is furniture that wants desperately to be noticed," Binzen confessed: "Bennett's pieces want to be more than mere furniture, and that's part of the problem I've always had with them—but it is also central to their appeal."[4] That is, to furniture world insiders like Binzen, it's an affront that Bennett's art is so showy, not at all demure and low-profile like much East Coast handmade furniture.

If Bennett is a hybrid artist, with one foot in the craft world and the other in the art world, he also makes hybrid objects, especially ones that cross between sculpture and painting, for example, seen in this exhibition. The *Wall Series* (pp. 70–75) takes iconic chairs by Michael Thonet (the *Café Chair*), deconstructs the original, full-scale readymade example and glues

Green Half Chair, 2006, enameled chair, 39" x 9 1/2" x 18"

Gerrit Rietveld (1888–1964)
© ARS, NY.
Red and Blue Chair, c. 1918
Wood, painted, 34 1/8 x 26 x 26 1/2".
Seat height: 13".
Gift of Philip Johnson. (487.1953)
The Museum of Modern Art, New York, NY, U.S.A.
Digital Image © The Museum of Modern Art/Licensed by SCALA/ Art Resource, NY
© 2006 Artists Rights Society (ARS), New York / Beeldrecht, Amsterdam

them to a flat, framed surface with a painted-on shadow of the chair. Toying with three-dimensional presence, illusionism, and light, these playful works push Bennett closer to Danto's camp, especially with their subdued colors. One work, though, *Green Half-Chair* (2006), shows particular promise for future exploration. Rather than framed, it blends into any adjacent wall, as if half-consumed by the wall space. Bennett's first site-related sculpture, *Green Half-Chair* claims the wall as its frame, rooting the piece in the real world, free of the somewhat self-conscious framing device of the other works in the series, or of a plinth or pedestal. If everything in Funk art is a joke of one sort or another, *Green Half-Chair* makes its point with a drier wit than is customary for Bennett.

When Bennett turned to the 18th-, 19th-, and 20th-century chair designers, he was stretching his critical purview as an artist more than ever before. Each figure has a historical weight. Duncan Phyfe is the godfather of American furniture and reproduction suburban dining room sets; Michael Thonet was the inventor of the Vienna Café Chair that launched political and cultural revolutions; and so on. The important thing to remember is how the original chairs are grace notes or starting points for a Bennett sculpture rather than sources of a faithful tribute or homage.

Thus, *GR series #3: "Duncan Rietveld"* (2003; p. 26) fuses a Duncan Phyfe seatback motif (similar to the famous optical illusion called the Rubens vase of two facing profiles) with an all-black Rietveld *Zig-Zag* chair of 1934. Spanning four centuries in one piece, it begins Bennett's odyssey, his design history demolition derby, with great sobriety and elegance.

Two riffs on the Morris chair, *Little Maurice* (2004; p. 57) and *Big Maurice* (2004) continue Bennett's friendly assault on chair history. With endearing modesty, Bennett commented on how he had "improved the original. It's a clumsy way to make the back go down," he noted of the ratcheted, adjustable easy chair.[5] Mechanical-appearing because of Morris's ambiguous relationship to the Industrial Revolution, the original Morris chair is given a startling makeover.

Equally uncomfortable, not to mention dangerous to sit on, Frank Lloyd Wright's hexagonal-backed side chair is travestied in *Wiggle Wright* (2004; p. 8). To Bennett, the Wright chair is "visually ugly, it's top heavy. His ego made him do it."[6] Knowing a thing or two about ego, Bennett's fearless assault continued rapidly throughout the next few years, mostly concentrating on the GR Series, Rietveld's *Zig-Zag Chair* variations, with increasing complexity and ingenuity.

Wright's near-contemporary, Charles Rennie Mackintosh, the Glasgow architect, further attenuated Morris's shapes for Scottish Arts and Crafts in his tall chairs. Literally adding a small stepladder to some different but related works, Bennett better comments upon Mackintosh in *GR series #5: "Chas Rietveld"* (2003; p. 25), with its cool white and dark green paint. The simple forms of the Rietveld design allow for Bennett's infinite sculptural extensions. This work's central element, the back, parodies the extreme height of Mackintosh's chairs.

Gerrit Rietveld (1888–1964)
© ARS, NY.
Zig-Zag Chair, 1934
Wood. Manufactured by G.A. Van de Groenekan, Amsterdam, The Netherlands, 29 x 14 7/8 x 16 ", seat h. 17".
Gift of Phyllis B. Lambert. (349.1966.vw3)
The Museum of Modern Art, New York, NY, U.S.A.
Digital image © The Museum of Modern Art/Licensed by SCALA/Art Resource, NY
© 2006 Artists Rights Society (ARS), New York / Beeldrecht, Amsterdam

Among the other works in the GR Series, several resist the double-artist references of the above works and address the Neo-Plastic severity of Rietveld's design more openly. *GR series #6: "Wing Chair"* (2003; cover) indulges in another pun, one not that far from the segmented back extensions of a traditional wing-back chair. Polished aluminum cut-out wing shapes are appended to a red-stained *Zigzag* format. *GR series #7: "Windsor"* (2003; p. 30) adds a small cushion to the basic Rietveld shape outlined in vermilion. As if to compensate at the last minute for such brevity, the artist bolted on custom-cut arms similar to those on a sack-back Windsor chair, archetypal chair of American antiques. Even simpler and most elegant of all, *GR series #10: "Chair-788"* (2003; p. 28) undulates all four planes of the Rietveld. The unexpected curves and sparing color re-invent the chair in ways that suggest a sculptural intervention of extreme delicacy and wit. At the same time, Bennett's softening of the brutal lines of the original is a virtual humanitarian act for the sitter's comfort.

GR series #4: "Granny Rietveld" (2003; p. 32) and *GR series #8: "Great Granny Rietveld"* (2003; p. 33) push potential comfort to new extremes. Part of a single-handed rescue effort for modern furniture's crimes, these chairs are subverting Bauhaus functionalism by introducing the one thing the moderns despised most in furniture: floral-patterned upholstery. Working with longtime upholsterer collaborator Jim Luque, Bennett first exhibited the upholstered *Zigzags* in a public preview at the Oakland Museum Sculpture Court, and then in a 2004 Boston exhibition at Gallery NAGA. Catalogue essayist John Dunnigan noted how, by violating such a taboo as floral upholstery, Bennett's chair "deftly combines the two archetypes of the avant-garde and the reactionary to create an object of transformative quality."[7] Restoring comfort as well as pattern to the Rietveld, Bennett renders the chair absurd, unexpected and contradictory.

One mid-century modern artist, furniture maker George Nakashima, also comes in for Bennett's affectionate dressing down. *Modified Nakashima* (2004; p. 59) and *Modernized Nakashima* (2004; p. 58) both grow out of Bennett's dissatisfaction with Nakashima's original design, a spindle-back that becomes the chair's only two legs supported by perpendicular rails on the floor. Bennett commented:

> I have never thought it was a very good-looking chair. That cantilever means a lot of trepidation, but it's a marvelous piece of engineering. . . In my versions, I've strengthened the sides. Now it's really strong. . . Much of [Nakashima's] work was very clunky but I've improved on it.[8]

While *Modernized Nakashima* is very sleek, *Modified Nakashima* retains the Japanese-American artist's use of highly figured wood.

Coming close to the present in his encyclopedia of modern design "improvements," Bennett also satirizes a single postmodern chair designer, Philippe Starck in *Granny Starck* (2004; p. 53) and *Stubby Starck* (2004: p. 52). These works also improbably add upholstery, in the process stripping away Starck's labored austerity of line.

George Nakashima
Conoid Chair, 1988
Walnut, ash, 20" x 21" x 35 1/2"
Collection of John and Robyn Horn
Photograph © Matt Bradley

Upholstered chair #2, 2001,
Steel chairs, plastic zip ties, powdercoat
35" x 20 1/2" x 24"

Chair for a Small Important Person, 2005,
rosewood, matte 23K gold-plated brass
and copper, Nautilus shell, pigmented
epoxy, etched steel, hand caned seat,
28 1/2" x 22 1/2" x 19"

Bennett next developed two other contrasting sets of sculptures, one based on imperial Chinese seating and the other on altered, mass-produced metal patio chairs. Having renovated modernist chair designs via Rietveld and others, Bennett next turned away from American furniture to bring us close to where the 21st century is situated today: facing China.

The legendary uncomfortable qualities of Chinese seating have much to do with class, hierarchy, authority, and status. Far from stand-ins for Everyman, Chinese chairs were for the person who could afford the chair and who would subsequently sit above everyone else in the room. With stretchers parallel to the ground and seats raised higher than expected, Chinese chairs were practical in that they raised the robes of the sitter above the muck on the floor.

First invited by curators at the nation's oldest history museum, the Peabody Essex Museum in Salem, Massachusetts, to participate in an exhibition that echoed or responded to classical Chinese furniture, "Inspired by China: Contemporary Furniture Makers Explore Chinese Traditions," Bennett created *Chair for a Small Important Person* (2005) and *Chinese Platform Chair #1: Late Oaktown Dynasty; 1934–____*; the former a squat form with enclosing armrests and shortened back, and the latter with a ziggurat back (a variation known as "Chinese cloud") and notched cushion. More reverent perhaps because of the exhibition's premise, Bennett quickly continued his encounters by creating a number of other platform chairs, his Late Oaktown Dynasty series. Ridiculing the rare and ostentatious Chinese woods often used in the original antiques, the use of softwood Douglas fir democratizes such objects as well as Americanizes them. They also constitute a fantasy of the new China, forward-looking but still bound to the past in many ways. They are possible seating for China's new elite, the international entrepreneurs and global capitalists. Caning plays an important role in the Late Oaktown Dynasty series and even rosewood puts in an appearance in *Chinese Platform Chair #4: Late Oaktown Dynasty; 1934-____* (2005; p. 68). Ornament is restored after the comparative austerities of the GR Series, in the form of mock medallions, found relief-carving panels, gold leaf, and other imperial appurtenances.

Finally, an earlier series touched upon but not pursued by Danto, shows great potential for Bennett to re-connect to Danto's genealogy of the altered readymade. Both *Upholstered Chair #1* (2001; p. 65) and *Upholstered Chair #2* (2002) are critiques of the aggressive character of suburban leisure. Stacking painted steel patio chairs and interweaving their metal lattice backs and seats with plastic electrical bundling ties, Bennett renders unseatable this most cherished of portable American chairs. *#1* uses primary colors that obliquely allude to Mondrian and to Rietveld's other signature chair, the *Blue and Red Chair* (1928: p. 12). Dazzling in its crisp linear filigree, *#1* celebrates but inhibits the amplitude of weekend pastimes. In reddish-orange, blue, and white, *#2* is a three-dimensional flag, a Fourth of July chair that comes to the party without a date, ready to engage the viewer without offering the comfort of seating. Bennett has intervened minimally compared to his extravagant works that followed, but has captured a moment in American middle-class culture that suggests the frantic nature of suburban leisure: so much to buy, so little time; so many design icons to acquire, so little space to display them in. Because of their stacking and weaving,

Upholstered Chairs #1 and *#2* remind us that, even with a lifetime of virtuoso studio techniques at his fingertips, it is the artist's critical eye scrutinizing the world around us that provides the impetus for his hybrid fusions of furniture and sculpture. They need not be art or craft; they are both. They need not choose between furniture and sculpture; they blend both in unforgettable ways.

Matthew Kangas
Independent art critic and curator
Seattle

[1] Table of Contents, *Woodshop News*, January 2006, 4.
[2] Arthur C. Danto, "Philosophizing with a Hammer," in Ursula Ilse-Neuman et al., *Made in Oakland: The Furniture of Garry Knox Bennett*. New York: American Craft Museum, 2001, 5-11.
[3] See my "Sculptural Heritage and Sculptural Implications: Turned Wood Objects in the Wornick Collection," in Tran Turner, et al., *Expressions in Wood: Masterworks from the Wornick Collection*. Oakland, Calif.: The Oakland Museum of California, 1996, 21-28.
[4] Jonathan Binzen, "Spectacular! Stirring! Fun!" *Woodwork*, October 2001, 31.
[5] Garry Knox Bennett, conversation with author, Oakland, California, March 2, 2006.
[6] Ibid.
[7] John Dunnigan, "Under Cover: Some Thoughts on Upholstered Furniture," in Arthur Dion, et al., *Under Cover: Upholstery in Contemporary Furniture*. Boston: Gallery NAGA.
[8] Garry Knox Bennett, conversation with author, Oakland, California, March 2, 2006.

GARRY KNOX BENNETT GETS IT IN THE END

GLENN ADAMSON

Is Garry Knox Bennett a fool, or a genius? Never having been a septuagenarian artist myself, it's hard to imagine what it would be like to be in his shoes. But I have a strong suspicion that only a man who has already played the game for decades could make the chairs he's been making for the past few years. True, Bennett has often skirted close to the brink of absurdity many times in his career. But never has he attacked a project so fearlessly. There is no sense that Bennett is trying to bring the vocabulary he is using under control. In their seemingly infinite variety, the chairs are untethered from any conceivable claim to a single design sensibility. For every example of jarring incoherence there is a work of careful unity; for every elegantly attenuated composition, a lumbering caricature; for every deadly serious formal exercise, a groaning pun; for every zig, a zag. While the chairs demonstrate Bennett's inexhaustible work ethic, his command of multifarious woodworking techniques, and his easy familiarity with furniture history, nobody who knows the artist would think that he cared a fig for any of those things, much less need to prove them.

No, the key to this body of work is that Bennett has, for the first time in his career, dared to make himself seem small. He has imported the massive weight of precedent into his studio, even being so bold as to include his own past signature motifs alongside the trademark forms of George Nakashima, Charles and Ray Eames, Michael Thonet, and the rest. Matthew Kangas, in his essay for this volume, argues that these chairs show Bennett to be a sculptor rather than a furnituremaker; that they ask us to "delight in the multiple layers of meaning, color, process and volume." This seems fair enough, but I can't shake the feeling that, in fact, the shifting reorganization of motifs in the chairs threatens to vacate the various colors, processes and volumes of any meaning. Sculptures these may be (more than 90 years after Marcel Duchamp, why not?), but collectively this series is as complete a statement about "chairness" as an irreducible, ineffable fact as an artist has ever cared to make. The overwhelming encyclopedic effect is similar to one of those Vitra posters of the Greatest 100

Thonet, 2004, chair, fiberglass, enamel paint, hand-caned seat, 34 1/2" x 25" x 17"

Sam Maloof
Rocker #60, 1982
Walnut, 45 1/2" x 25 3/4" x 44 3/4"
White House Collection of American Crafts
Photograph © John Bigelow Taylor

Chair Designs Of The 20th Century which intimidates so many beginning designers in art schools across the country—only more so. There is no "greatest" chair here, no preference given to any one historical reference point over another. Every permutation seems to have been carried out, as if Bennett had not allowed himself to edit the combinatorial possibilities.

In retrospect, it seems inevitable that the chair would have become the subject for Bennett's delirious experiment. The idea presents him with a relatively clean slate, for one thing, in that the chair is the one major furniture type that he has never really nailed (so to speak) in his long career. The one notable series of chairs he executed previously, which were African-inspired affairs hung with beads, did not entirely capture his own or the public's imagination. They seemed mainly to confirm the fact that his planar, imagistic style was more suited to tables and case furniture than to chairs, which demand to be considered in three dimensions. The task of designing a chair is all about nuance. The exact curves of arm and seat, the precise angles at which the back extends into space and the legs meet the floor, are what make a chair design a success or a failure. While Bennett can be capable of surprising delicacy when he wants to, such fussy calculations are not his natural métier.

There was, then, a conspicuous gap in Bennett's otherwise bulletproof résumé that only an iconic chair design could fill. This was perhaps a dilemma for him, in the sense that great furnituremakers tend to be judged by their chairs, not their sideboards. I've elsewhere argued that each of the crafts has its own key form, which tends to stand in metonymically for both an individual maker's career and for a craft in general. For furnituremakers that form is inevitably the chair. In historical memory, the Chippendale side chair, the Eames LCW Chair, and the Sam Maloof rocker far outshine the tables or cabinets associated with those names. This is probably because furniture, unlike the other crafts, typically exists on human scale and engages the whole body, and the chair does this most directly. Jewelers, similarly, are best symbolized by the brooch, because it is the most elemental way to ornament the body. For potters it's the teapot, which appeals for its language of containment and its inherently asymmetrical composition. Weavers, whose looms impose two-dimensionality to an extent unusual in the other crafts, make wall hangings so that they can flirt with the condition of painting. Glassmakers, who have by and large shown a propensity towards visual appeal rather than conceptual inquiry, have the vase, which just stands in the window and looks pretty.

At any rate, furnituremakers have chairs to worry about, and Bennett has never really solved the problem. Even the new chairs aren't that different from the ones he has made in the past, compositionally speaking. Though tremendously diverse as a group, each one is a collision of four flattish elements at right angles (the two sides, back, and seat). While this underlying planarity may simply reflect Bennett's intuitive design sense, it also connotes the Postmodern in no uncertain terms. The discrete elements of the chairs—an easily recognized back here, an eccentric gesture of an arm there—are deployed as free-floating signs. Were one teaching an art history lesson on the Postmodern chair, one might begin with the equally flat, laminate-sheathed compositions of designers like Peter Shire, Ettore Sottsass, and Robert Venturi, and continue through the 1980s work of studio furnituremakers such as Wendy Maruyama's

Wendy Maruyama
Mickey Mackintosh, 1982
Wood, zolotone, 65" x 29" x 19"
Collection of Garry and Sylvia Bennett
Image © San Francisco Museum of Craft + Design

Tom Loeser
Folding Chair, 1988
Wood, stainless steel, aluminum, paint,
34" x 25" x 22"
Courtesy of the artist.
Photograph © Dean Powell

Monarch Oil Can "Lion head," 1996.
Can, aluminum, epoxy, lamp parts,
14" x 6 1/4" x 8 1/2". Private collection

Mickey Mackintosh, Tom Loeser's *Folding Chairs*, Alphonse Mattia's animated valet chairs, and Wendell Castle's sculptural *Angel* series. A good choice for the more tasteful cultural hybridization of the 1990s might be Kristina Madsen, who grafts Fijian chip-carving onto Neoclassical shapes; or perhaps one might opt for an object that reflects the darker side of globalization, such as Tejo Remy's *Rag Chair*. Whatever path one took, though, one would almost certainly want to end with Bennett's chairs. All the familiar tropes of the Postmodern are on display, and at fever pitch. There is historic quotation; compositional pastiche; thick irony; and above all, an insistence on the equivalence, even the interchangeability, of heterogeneous and even antithetical styles. This is Postmodernism in its High Baroque phase, inflated to be sure, but still good for one last big bang.

The chairs compare closely with Bennett's only previous series of similarly manic scale, his *100 Lamps* (made for a show at Peter Joseph Gallery in 1996). When I interviewed Bennett a few years ago, he conceded that there were no "lasting images" from that project, and yet also claimed (in his typically cagey way) that it was his "crowning achievement." In retrospect though, for all their ingenuity, the lamps now seem like they were just a warm-up act. Partly this is just a matter of scale. The lamps, which were quickly assembled from assorted *objets trouvés*, could be made out to be winning but negligible whimsies. The chairs on the other hand, because of their size and intrinsic anthropomorphism, command attention. Even if this mismatched chorus line of objects was composed in a process of inspired free-association—like a sketchbook come to life—it seems, at the same time, to be definitive of something.

What it comes down to, I think, is that Bennett has finally called his own bluff. The project is Quixotic in the extreme: it thrusts design greatness of every stripe at us, practically pleading with us to see Bennett's own moment (and by extension, our own) as a state of fallen grace, in which quotation and derivativeness are all that remains. And yet, Bennett seems to be suggesting that we might want to pause in this moment and revel in the freedom of the state of affairs. For all of the superficially adolescent quality of these chairs (their undigested ideas, their rough humor, their sheer energy), they are nonetheless deeply mature works, which cast a raking light on Bennett's uncertain place in furniture history. Apparently, he has made peace with the idea that he is fundamentally a Postmodernist, which is to say, a poacher. Unlike the grand self-sufficiency of a Modernist designer, like Gerrit Rietveld, Bennett's best moments have always been relational—not always critical, but nearly always reactive. Now he has declared this in himself: made it clear that he is a magpie artist whose greatest talent lies not in creating things from scratch, but in putting them together cockeyed. This taking of accounts must have taken some serious courage, for he has now situated himself firmly at the butt end of furniture history. A foolish thing to do? Perhaps, but that of course is the genius of it. If you're Garry Knox Bennett, it makes sense to ensure that you'll have the final word.

Glenn Adamson
Deputy Head of Research and Head of Graduate Studies
Victoria and Albert Museum

ONE ARTWORK OR TWO:
NAIL CABINET AND ITS NO-FRILLS SHIPPING CASE

ARTHUR C. DANTO

Garry Knox Bennett's 1979 *Nail Cabinet* is a masterwork of fine cabinetry deliberately vandalized by its maker for the purpose of calling into question the ideal of fine cabinetry it otherwise exemplifies. The vandalism consisted in driving into the front of the cabinet a large nail that violates the code of joinery that governs work of this quality; bending it in violation of the skill the cabinetmaking otherwise demonstrates; and pounding it into the finely finished surface of the cabinet's rare veneer, leaving some dents behind. It was an act of insurrection and repudiation, a declaration of artistic independence, a protest against a stultifying practice, a blow struck for the principle of aesthetic freedom in a domain that had made a prison of rules that had turned imagination into its inmate. It hammered down a wall that had limited the art of furniture-making, opening a new era in which the boundary between craft and art was breached. It became an iconic manifesto that wordlessly claimed the status of artist for those who had been stigmatized as mere artisans. Inevitably it became a legend, and something everyone interested in the new order it had established wanted to see.

In consequence of this demand, *Nail Cabinet* became an itinerant prophet, making its way from venue to venue, diverting a disproportionate amount of studio time and effort from the artistic creativity it was supposed to have liberated, to the labor of crating and shipping, and exposing *Nail Cabinet* to wear, tear, and degradation. Its proclamatory nail was actually stolen on one occasion. Because of its particular notoriety and star status, moreover, *Nail Cabinet* distracted the artist's time and energy from other work in which he was interested. It had, not to put too fine a point on it, made its point. The moment had come to think of other matters.

It was on a recent return of *Nail Cabinet* from one of its journeys, while it stood, waiting to be uncrated, that Garry Knox Bennett was struck by the aesthetics of what the French call *emballage* – the craft of wrapping and packing. *Nail Cabinet* stood half-exposed on the workshop floor, its protected delicate self contrasting with the robust carpentry of its stout container.

Nail Cabinet, 1979, paduk, glass, lamp parts, copper, wood, 96" x 48" x 24"(crated)

The aesthetics of contrast between the rough container and the elegant contained all at once awakened a new idea in the same mind that had originated the brilliant message of *Nail Cabinet* many years earlier. Why not *leave* it there? Why not display it securely ensconced in its efficient housing of wood and Styrofoam, screwed together and embellished with red instructions to its handlers? And with this a solution to the problem of *Nail Cabinet*'s destiny recommended itself. Many museums would love to have *Nail Cabinet* for its collections. Let any museum that agrees to exhibit it, visible through openings in its shipping crate, have, upon the occasion of the artist's death, the first right to purchase the work, and consummate its ownership by unpacking this famous object. One thinks immediately of Duchamp's notorious work—*The Bride Stripped Bare by Her Bachelors, Even*.

The actual terms of transfer must be negotiated by lawyers skilled in drafting watertight documents. Everyone benefits. The artist benefits by surrendering responsibility for a burdensome work, having guaranteed an institutional home for his most famous product. His estate benefits. The museum benefits. And the philosophy of art benefits by inheriting a new problem. Is the object that consists of *Nail Cabinet* together with its packaging one artwork or two? And if two, will it be vandalism to destroy the container? Will *Nail Cabinet* just look vulnerable and naked, divested of the covering that kept it safe, secure, and sheltered? Or will its public miss the hybrid being that consisted in fine cabinetry and rough carpentry?

Arthur C. Danto
Art critic, professor and philosopher

PLATES

GR series #5: "Chas Rietveld," 2003, enameled wood, nickel-plated brass, 54 1/2" x 15" x 17 1/8"

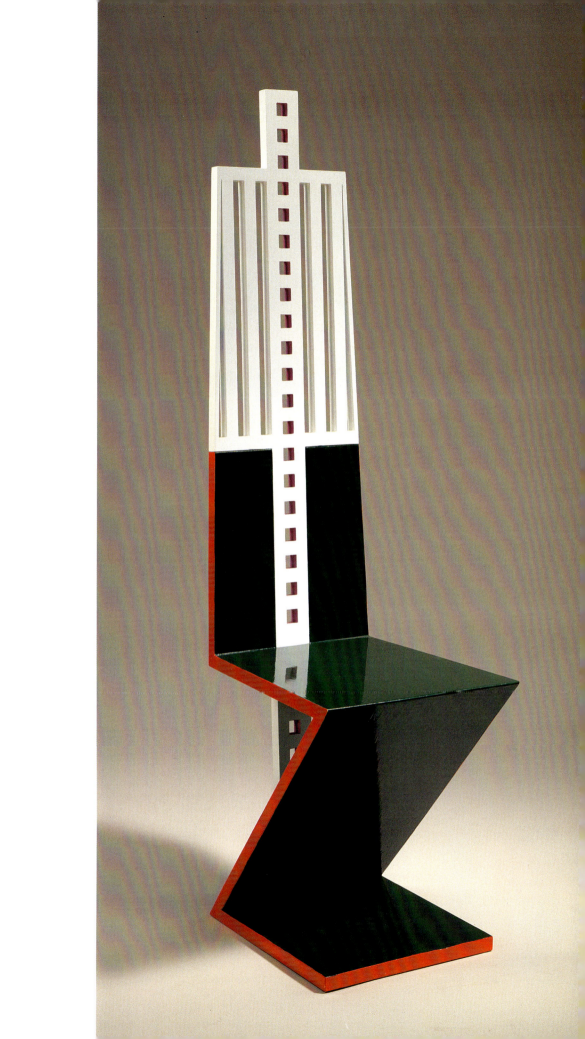

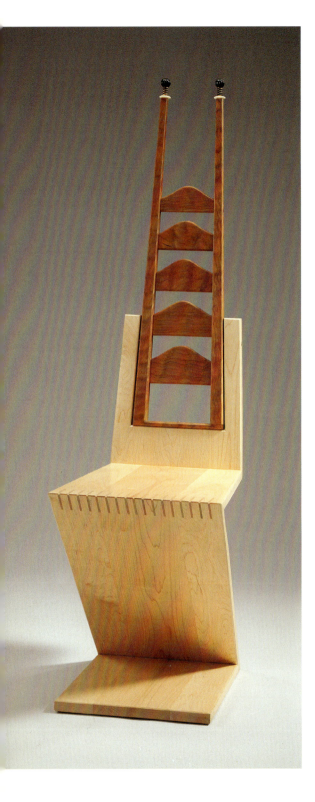 

(left) *GR series #2:* "Old Ladderback," 2003, maple, cherry, bone, beads, copper, 51 1/2" x 14 5/8" x 17 1/4"

(right) *GR series #3:* "Duncan Rietveld," 2003, dyed mahogany, lacewood, 23K gold-plated brass, 39 5/8" x 14 3/4" x 17 1/2"

(opposite) *GR series #1:* "New Ladderback," 2003, maple, Douglas fir, nickel-plated brass, GKB fabricated ladder, 41 3/4" x 14 5/8" x 22"

GR series #10: "Chair-788," 2003, lacquered wood, yellow satinwood, 29 1/8" x 15 1/4" x 15 3/4"

(opposite) *GR series #14:* "XYZ Chair," 2003, lacquered wood, aluminum, 33 1/2" x 15" x 18"

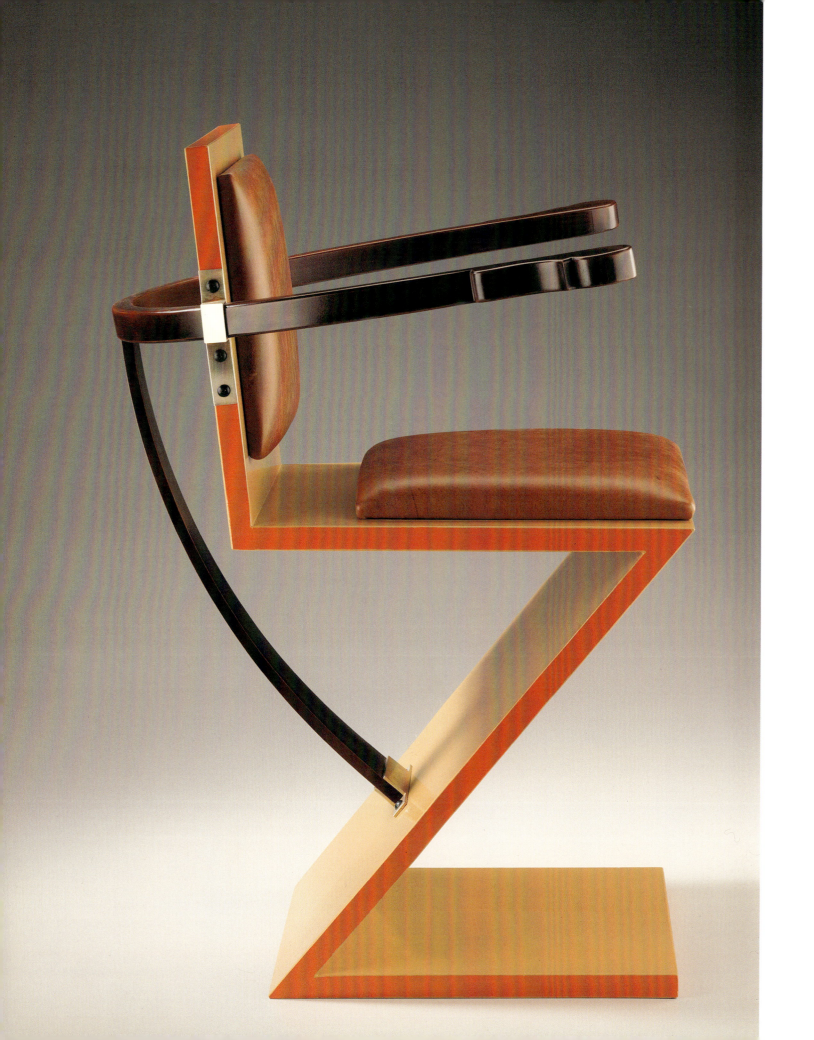

(opposite) *GR series #7:* "Windsor," 2003, enameled wood, lacquered wood, upholstered leather, silver-plated brass, 30" x 23 1/2" x 22 1/4"

(above) *GR series #11:* "Chair-789," 2003, yellow cedar, pigmented epoxy, 29 1/2" x 14 3/4" x 17"

(right) *GR series #13:* "Chair-791, 2003," lacquered cherry, G-10, 23K gold-plated brass, 31 1/2" x 14 1/2" x 19 1/2"

(left) *GR series #4:* "Granny Rietveld," 2003, red oak, hand-caned seat, polished brass, 33 3/4" x 17" x 17 1/8"

(right) *GR series #9:* "Early Twentieth Century Chair," 2003, lacquered wood and plywood, 32 1/4" x 14 7/8" x 18 3/4"

(opposite) *GR series #8:* "Great Granny Rietveld," 2003, wood, upholstered cotton, 30 3/4" x 15" x 18"

GR series #12: "Chair-790," 2003, cherry, polished brass, 32" x 14 1/2" x 16 1/2"

(opposite) *GR series #15:* "Thong," 2003, Douglas fir, cherry, paint, 34 1/2" x 18 3/4" x 17 1/4"

(left) *Prototype series #1,* 2004, shellacked wood, gouache, 23K gold-plated brass, 32" x 20" x 20 1/2"

(right) *Prototype series #4:* "Joe's Chair," 2003, painted wood, aluminum, upholstered canvas duck, 21 1/2" x 21 1/2" x 22 1/2"

(opposite) *Prototype series #3,* 2003, painted wood, upholstered canvas duck, 23K gold-plated brass, stainless steel wire, 29 1/2" x 18" x 22"

Sylvia's Chair, 2004, lacquered wood, hand-caned seat, 31" x 22" x 25"

Chair-900, 2006, 23K gold leafed wood, yellow satinwood, pigmented epoxy, upholstered velvet, 26" x 21" x 24"

(opposite) *Chair-881*, 2005, lacquered wood, figured maple, white oak, machine-caned seat, upholstered leather, brass, 34 3/4" x 23 1/2" x 25"

(left) *Chair-858*, 2004, lacquered wood, white oak, G-10, gouache, brass, pigmented epoxy, 33 1/4" x 20 1/2" x 26"

(right) *Chair-851*, 2004, enameled wood, mahogany, lacquered G-10, 32" x 26" x 26"

(opposite) *Chair-883*, 2005, maple, machine-caned seat, upholstered leather, gouache on plywood, 35" x 23" x 28"

Chair-885, 2005, maple, upholstered cotton, 28" x 20" x 26"

(opposite) *Chair-886*, 2005, enameled wood, machine caned seat, 31" x 18" x 24"

Chair-857, 2004, enameled wood, upholstered leather, G-10, 23K gold-plated brass, 31 1/4" x 19 1/2" x 23 1/2"

Yellow Satinwood with Blue, 2004, yellow satinwood, lacquer, 23K gold-plated brass, leather upholstery, 40" x 26 1/2" x 30"

(opposite) *Chair-912*, 2005, wood, paint, upholstered embossed leather, 31" x 22 1/2" x 25"

(opposite) *Chair-887*, 2005, walnut, matte silver-plated copper, upholstered embossed leather, Formica ColorCore®, 32 3/4" x 27 1/2" x 32"

Scroll Chair, 2005, dyed walnut, brass, synthetic leather upholstery, 37" x 25" x 32 1/2"

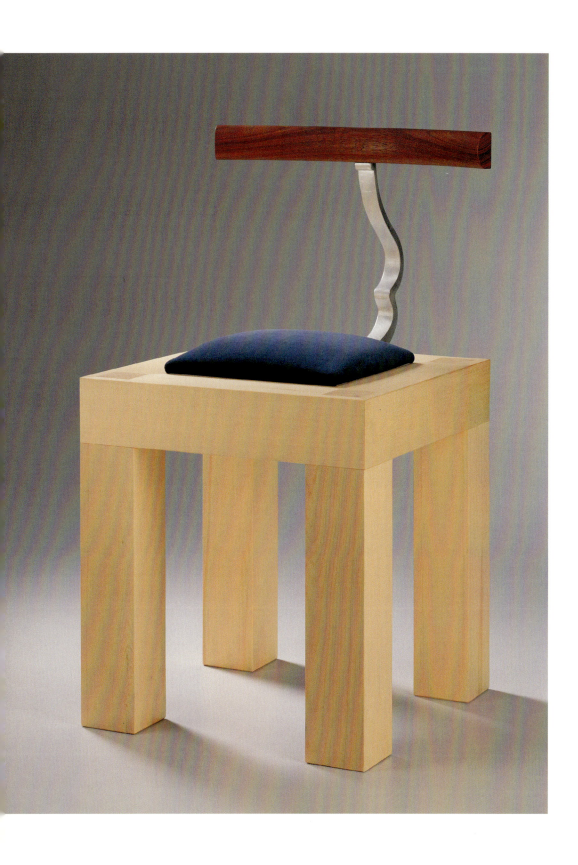

Stubby Starck, 2004, yellow cedar, aluminum, upholstered velvet, 29" x 16" x 22"

(opposite) *Granny Starck*, 2004, yellow cedar, lacquered wood, aluminum, upholstered leather, 31" x 16" x 32"

Reitveld Redux, 2004, painted wood, beads, 33 1/4" x 24" x 20 1/4"

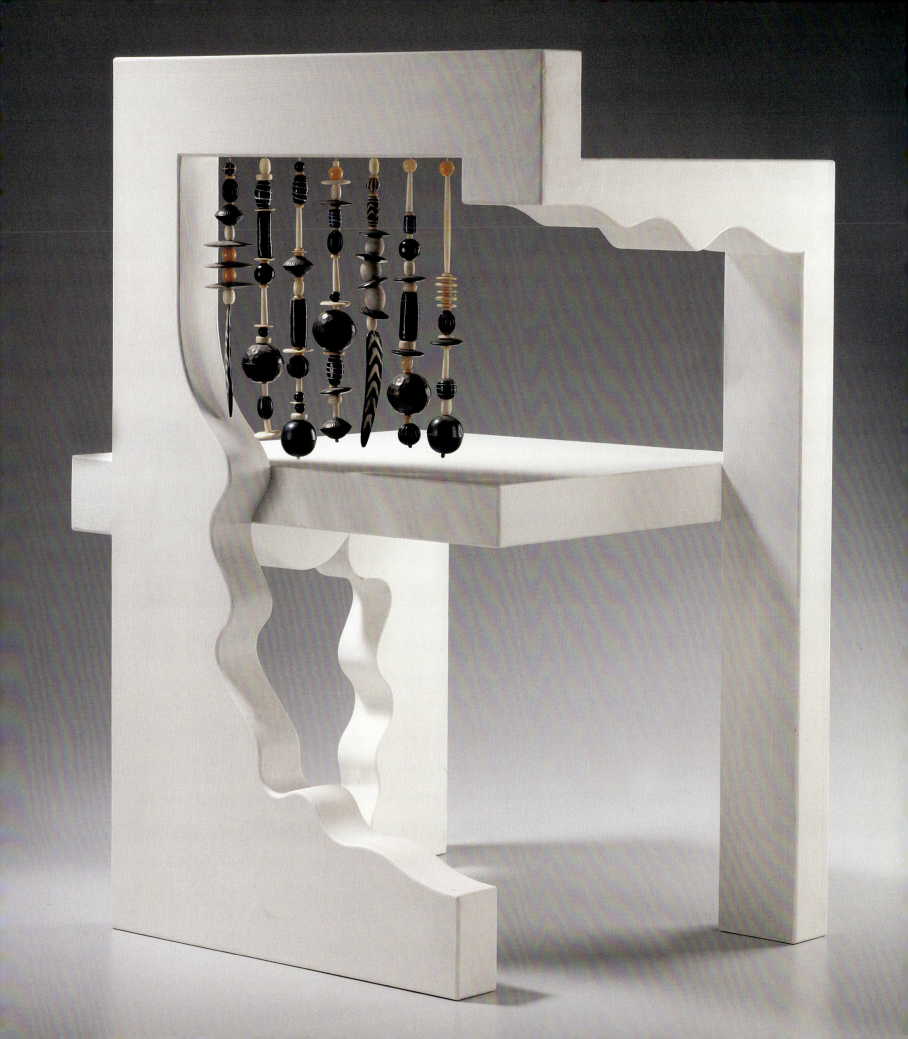

Little Maurice, 2004, mahogany, polished brass, upholstered faux alligator leather, 38 1/2" x 27 1/2" x 30"

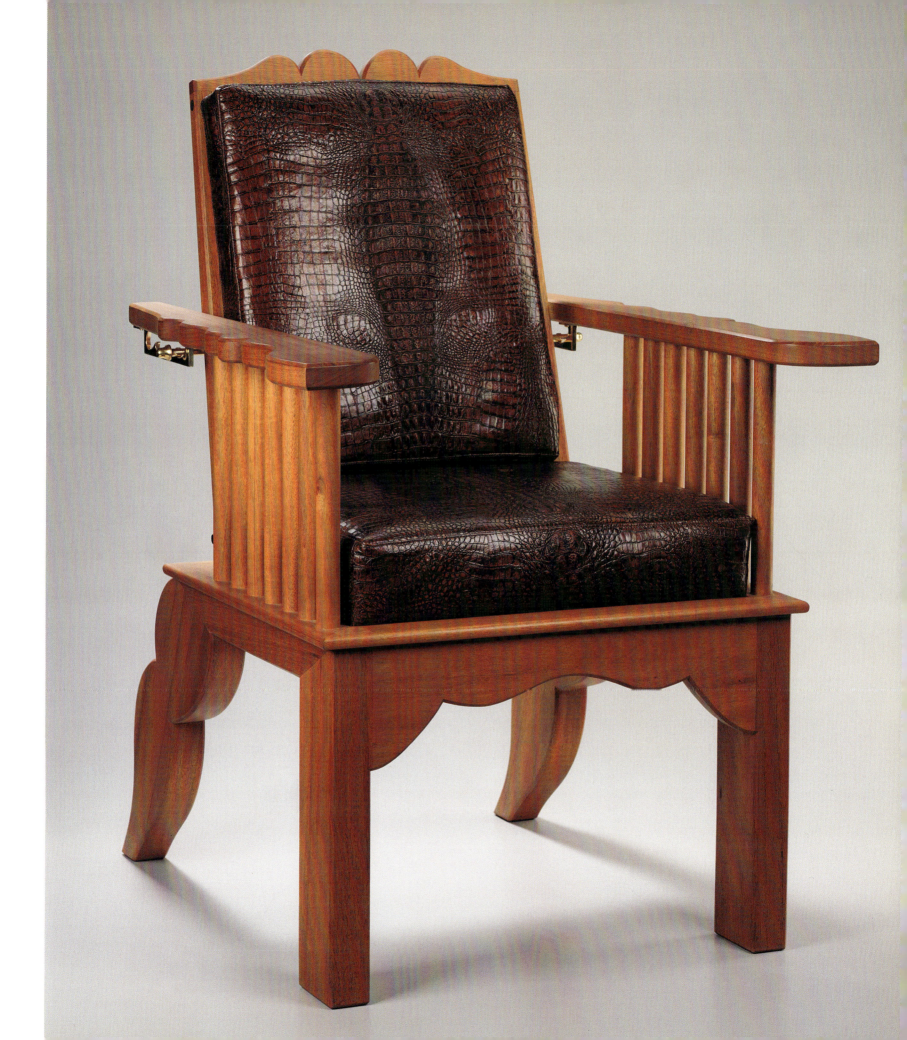

Modernized Nakashima, 2004, mahogany, polished brass, 36 1/4" x 18 1/2" x 24"

(opposite) *Modified Nakashima*, 2004, Oregon walnut, 35" x 19 1/4" x 23 1/2"

#1 Gord, 2004, mixed hardwood, 51" x 25" x 24"

Char, 2004, California black walnut, Douglas fir, washboard, copper, 38 3/4" x 15 1/4" x 16"

(opposite) *#2 Gord, Mark, Gupta*, 2004, mixed exotic wood, carved Indian panel, 45 1/2" x 24 1/2" x 27 1/2"

Upholstered chair #1, 2001, powdercoat, steel chairs, plastic zip ties, 35" x 20 1/2" x 24"

Chair Drawing With 2 Cushions, 2004, plastic chair, steel wire, cement, paint, 34 1/2" x 22" x 24"

(opposite) *Martha Stewart Chair*, 2004, plastic chair, lacquered white oak, cotton upholstery, 35" x 22" x 25"

Chinese Platform Chair #4: Late Oaktown Dynasty; 1934– ____., 2005, rosewood, hand-caned seat, polished brass, 43" x 25" x 26"

(opposite) *Chinese Platform Chair #2: Late Oaktown Dynasty; 1934– ____.*, 2005, lacquered wood, pigmented epoxy, bamboo, velvet upholstery, 39" x 22 3/4" x 25 1/2"

Thonet wall series 1/4, 2006, chair, wood panel, paint, 47 1/2" x 36 1/2" x 12 1/2"

Thonet wall series 2/4, 2006, chair, wood panel, paint, 47 1/2" x 36 1/2" x 12 1/2"

(opposite) *Thonet wall series 3/4*, 2006, chair, wood panel, paint, 47 1/2" x 36 1/2" x 12 1/2"

Thonet wall series 4/4, 2006, chair, wood panel, paint, 47 1/2" x 36 1/2" x 12 1/2"

(opposite) *Thonet wall Chair-908*, 2006, chair, wood panel, paint, 48" x 39" x 12 1/4"

GARRY KNOWS BEST

A CONVERSATION WITH THE ARTIST

STEFANO CATALANI

I met with Garry Knox Bennett in his studio in Oakland, California. There—surrounded by his chairs; a selection of paintings by Ambrose Pillphister;[1] a large erotic painting of Japonisme-revival flavor; cabinets; tables; bibelots; and chairs by furnituremaker-friends—we spoke of his attitude toward his recent and past work.

What emerged from our conversation was the artist's wholehearted dedication to the design process by means of sampling an existing vocabulary of forms and ideas from others; his departure from obeying the aesthetics of wood; and his pursuit to link furniture to the spheres of fine arts and sculpture.[2]

The value Bennett gives to the use of color and line underpins this venture, for the chair is for him what the canvas is for the painter. His carefully chosen colors establish a pictorial network of working relationships among the design elements of the chair to set the "temperature" of the composition. A comment of his during our interview measures the stature of this undertaking: If I had Frank Stella's ability to put color on something, I'd be the greatest furnituremaker of our time. Bennett treats not only the designs of Wright, Mackintosh, and Stark, but also works by Stella and Rauschenberg as paragons in his furnituremaking! His chairs provide an intellectual intimacy with the visual experimentations and solutions of his predecessors, which sets his work in the continuum of history of design and art of the last century and half.

Bennett elevates the chair from the floor of functionality to the domain of the sculptural by asserting the autonomous dimension of the surface from its chairness. Such a liberation of the surface is crucial for experiencing the chair as 3-D object not only bound to style and comfort, but also in its pure existence of form in space and light.

GARRY KNOX BENNETT: Ask your questions in Italian. *Questione!* Is that right?

STEFANO CATALANI: *Domanda.*

GKB: *Questione!*

SC: *Questione* means problem. *Domanda* means question.

GKB: *Domanda*, huh? *Domanda!*

SC: In the interview conducted by Glenn Adamson for the Smithsonian Institution's Archives of American Art, on February 1 and 2, 2002, here in Oakland, you mentioned a desire to do a chair series…since you had "some cat's-ass ideas for chairs" —

GKB: Yeah! Cat's ass!

SC: Four years later, the exhibition *Garry Knox Bennett: Call Me Chairmaker*, featuring fifty-two new chairs from a series of more than eighty will open at Bellevue Arts Museum in July 2006. You have always been devoted to pursuing your ideas using the series format. When did you start working on this series?

GKB: I don't know. I started on chairs right after our house in Alameda burned down, right Sylvia? May 13, 2003. Well, I wanted to get right to work because my head was occupied, and everything was smoked up and wet. I think it was just a way to get busy.

SC: You started with your *Zigzag* chairs, eventually making sixteen, drawing inspiration from the design of Gerrit Rietveld's 1934 *Zig-Zag Chair*. It's a quite spartan chair in its original concept. What captured your interest about this model?

Chair-915, 2006, Douglas fir, enameled wood, 34" x 20" x 23"

---

[1] Painter Ambrose Pillphister is one of Garry Knox Bennett's alter egos.
[2] Bennett couldn't be a better fit with what Edward S. Cooke, Jr. evinced when portraying the second generation of furnituremakers in his 1989 survey; Edward S. Cooke, Jr., *New American Furniture, The Second Generation of Studio Furnituremakers*, Museum of Fine Arts, Boston, 1989, page 10.

GKB: I've always looked at that chair as kind of a joke. I thought, "What a dumb chair this is!" And when I made the first, the ladderback chair, which started out as kind of tongue-in-cheek, I sat in it, and it was a surprisingly comfortable little chair! I mean it works really well. You can get your feet behind it, when you tuck your feet under yourself; there's no stretcher that gets in the way. It's a good height: 18 inches, pretty standard. And it's got some spring to it; it's got a little limber to it. So then I have to admit, I actually fell in love with the model. From then on, I was fairly serious. Obviously I'm using puns in a lot of the titles, or a lot of visuals, but I got pretty serious about it.

SC: Did you build all the *Zigzag* chairs? Or are some of them Garry Knox Bennett's "readymades" in the sense that you began working with an original Rietveld?

GKB: Purchasing original Rietveld *Zig-Zag* chairs would be a pretty expensive proposition. I don't even know anybody who's manufacturing them. But it's a very easy chair to construct. It's unbelievably simple.

SC: A lot of dovetail joints…

GKB: Yeah, but I modified it. I think in most cases, my engineering is better… I mean, they put dovetails in that real hard angle; I don't even know who could make that dovetail. But they did, and they support it with gussets. I never saw a real Rietveld, but in all the pictures I saw, they had nuts and bolts in them, or they had these gussets stuck in them or battens. Instead of dovetails I used a spline joint: I set up a jig for the table saw, and sawed through the wood. I think there's anywhere from twelve to maybe fifteen splines across. Then I milled down a piece of wood that fits in that slot, glued it in there really good, then sanded it all down even.

SC: What kind of wood did you use for your *Zigzag* chairs?

GKB: Any wood that was available. The wood wasn't important. For *Wing Chair* I used lacewood. I foot-matched it so that you have that stripe running all the way down through it.

SC: Rietveld's *Zig-Zag Chair* design is a stark and minimal assertion of function and form: four planes in space, four straight lines in profile. Did you fall in love with its lines?

GKB: It's such a simple form that it allows itself a lot of manipulation. It's an easy form to build off visually and physically: color, or what you can stick on it, like the wings or the ladder, or the Mackintosh high back. If you want, make it into an armchair!

SC: The first two *Zigzag* chairs you made are *GR series #2: "Old Ladderback"* (p. 26) and *GR series #1: "New Ladderback"* (p. 27) —

GKB: Right, I had in mind the Shaker ladderback.

SC: You started off with the classic Shaker style, one of the earliest and most popular American designs —

GKB: I just didn't want to make a Rietveld chair. I was going to do something with it.

And everything just happened from that.

SC: After the Shaker-inspired *Old Ladderback* and *New Ladderback*, you made the *GR series #3: "Duncan Rietveld,"* (p. 26) which is inspired by Duncan Phyfe.

GKB: And that's an easy shape to do. There's no carving in it, you know. I tried to find somebody who could carve me the back splat, the cherubs. I wanted something really gaudy. I found one guy who would do it, but then he asked, "What are you going to do with it?" I explained to him and he didn't want his work messed with. So, I could do it, if I could learn how to sharpen a chisel.

SC: You have said that many times in the past.

GKB: Yeah, I know, but they're hard to sharpen. Some people can sharpen 'em real quick. Wendell Castle can sharpen a chisel in about five minutes. I could carve something, but it would take *forever*, and the whole idea here, as in most of my work, is not to lavish a lot of time on this stuff. We're just talking ideas here.

SC: Your *GR series #5: "Chas Rietveld"* (p. 25) is one of my favorite pieces. There is such an integration *and* compatibility. The quintessential elements of Charles Rennie Mackintosh design are so well integrated with the *Zig-Zag Chair*. The two designs come together in the simplest, seamless way: almost obvious!

GKB: Yeah, that is pretty clever, isn't it? The white bar goes all the way to the base, and that makes a real strong chair. You could sit a 500-pound guy in that chair.

SC: You gave a technical and psychological solution to the main concern one has when one sits in the original *Zig-Zag Chair* —

GKB: Oh, of course, that it's going to hold.

SC: What do you think of Mackintosh's designs for furniture?

GKB: Another architect making furniture for Christ's sake. It's elegant, beautiful stuff, and is probably uncomfortable as hell. You know, there isn't an architect in the world who can make chairs. They don't understand chairs. You know? I haven't seen an architect chair yet that's worth a shit…well other than those by Le Corbusier and Charles Eames…

SC: And yet you had already paid homage to Mackintosh in the past.

GKB: Yeah. The *Mackintosh Bench*.

SC: It's interesting, the first thing one would look for when looking at the bench would be any obvious reference to the austere elements of Mackintosh design: the high back, the grid, or the semicircular forms—

GKB: The colors! Mackintosh loved mauve. The bench had mauve. And mauve is the color I painted inside the square holes of the white bar on the back of *Chas Rietveld*.

SC: As you said with your *Zigzag* chairs, you mainly play on two different levels: the literal pun and the visual joke. *GR series #4: "Granny Rietveld"* (p. 32), *GR series #8: "Great Granny Rietveld"* (p. 33), and *GR series #15: "Thong"* (p. 35) are hilarious, but there are some *Zigzag* chairs in which you just relish the possibilities offered by the chair's original simplicity and intrinsic graphic quality —

GKB: *XYZ*, right there!

SC: Right: the *GR series #14: "XYZ Chair"* (p. 29).

GKB: The *y* lends itself awfully good to a backrest, the *x* is just kind of hidden, but that chair is really strong.

SC: And what about the colors? You like to use color.

Mackintosh Bench, 1981
Redwood, fir, automotive lacquer, 20" x 60" x 16".
Collection of Michael and Louise Stone.
Photograph © Garry Knox Bennett Archive

GKB: I try. I work at it very hard when I decide to color something. I really spend a lot of thought. It's not like "Oh I'll just put a little red." And that's the problem with a lot of furniture I see that young people do. "Oh, red, blue, yellow, green." You know there's value to the color: warm, cool, and how they relate to each other. But when I take the paint to cover the wood, see it's kind of goofy because I say, "Yeah, I don't care about the wood; I paint it." But I spend so much intellectual energy on what color the paint is. It's still not free yet. I'm just so conservative in a way, you know.

SC: Conservative?

GKB: Yeah, insofar as when I make something, there's still a preciousness about it in my own mind. "God, I put all this labor… don't do something crazy." But the paint, if I have any fucking *cajones* at all, I may take that chair and pour a bucket of paint on it. But I'm sitting here and I want to do it because I want to see it, but, you know what that does? That's so premeditated. Good art is not really premeditated. It would be better if one day I was just down in my shop and said "Aw, geez, I just made another of these cute chairs; where's that bucket of paint?" Now that would be a statement. That would be Rauschenberg's goat [in his *Monogram* of 1959]. In my 1979 *Nail Cabinet*, in one of the drawers I wrote on the bottom: if the tire fucked up

Rauschenberg's goat, so the nail fucks the cabinet up. But you and I will know, and this audio tape, which you'll save, we'll both know that then it was really premeditated. But it's still a good idea, and I'll save it. Anyway, for the *XYZ Chair*, I dyed the wood black first, then I started playing. You look at that maroon against that grey and the yellow …those are really *good* colors. I mean they work really well.

SC: With *GR series #6: "Wing Chair"* (cover), you perfectly replicated Rietveld's *Zig-Zag Chair*, and then you mounted the two aluminum wings, which is one of Garry Knox Bennett's signature designs.

GKB: A lot of times people make really complicated things and they end up sticking embellishment *on* the object. I try to incorporate it, whether it be structural or decorative. You know, the wings are in! I milled out the slots with a router. So, you know I didn't just screw them on the back. That would look cheesy (American term there).

SC: The free form of the wings makes such a graphic contrast with the rigid linearity of the chair.

GKB: I'm very careful. If I'm doing something that has curves in it, I'm very careful not to make it all curved. I want to throw some hard lines in there, or if I'm making something very rectilinear, I want to throw curves in it, as in the handle on the top of the *Deck Chair* [*GR series #12: "Chair-790"*] (p. 34). You know, just some curve. Because there are no curves in that piece, and you just want to, I always need to do that.

SC: Your *Zigzag* chairs were just the overture to the whole series. You had worked in series in the past: lamps —

GKB: …clocks…

SC: — the *Tablelamps*…

GKB: …jewelry.

SC: The series format seems then to offer the widest spectrum of possibilities for your creativity.

GKB: Yeah, because the ideas feed on each other. I'm pretty sure when I'm working on a piece, I already know what it's going to look like. Sure there are some changes—color for example—but now it's just work. So, I'm already thinking of the next piece.

SC: Why?

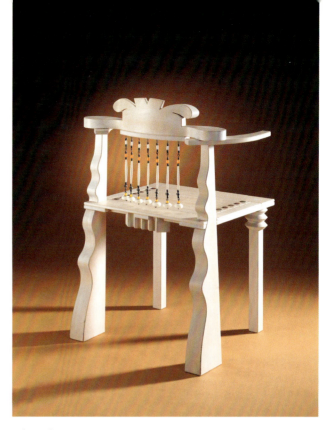

White Chair, 1989
Maple, watercolor, beads, 32 3/4" x 21" x 19"
Collection of Fletcher and Bobbie Benton

GKB: I have more ideas than time. And I get bored with what I'm doing, I mean, once the idea takes shape, I am over it, *but* I gotta finish it! If I had a magic wand, I'd fill this place up in ten minutes and then we'd ship it out. We'd sell it on the street $3 a piece. People would get some good stuff and tomorrow I'd put a bunch more out.

SC: Excellent stuff —

GKB: Oh, I'm a good craftsman, well…pretty good craftsman. But there are people much better than me. I can do that type of work, but it takes so much time, and why make it perfect?

SC: Going back to the chair topic and the series approach, you had already done chairs during the 1980s.

GKB: Yeah. The *African* chairs [*White Chair*, above]. But they were not a series. They were one design that I adhered to the physical shape of, the measurements and everything, but changed the woods and the bead patterns. It's just one chair interpreted forty-seven different ways. For each of the *African* chairs, the measurements, but not the inspiration, came from the Thonet bentwood chair, *Model #233 P*, which is perfect. It's 18 to 19 inches from the floor. The

The Thonet bentwood chair *Model 233 P* in Garry Knox Bennett's studio. Photograph © Alison McLennan

backrest is up to 12 inches. It's open to the back so your coccyx can get out, and the armrests are at the right height. It's one of the best chairs ever designed. It's comfortable. It's simple. Because I had to take classes in chairmaking and theory. No, really, stuff like that. I mean there are chairmakers who know all the theory. They know how high the arms should be, where the backrest should hit you.

SC: You took painting and sculpture in college.

GKB: That's right. I didn't take chair.

SC: Getting back to Rietveld's designs, *Rietveld Redux* is another chair in the current series inspired by another one of Rietveld's concept chairs.

GKB: Yeah. The *Steltman Chair*.

SC: As with your *GR series #5: "Chas Rietveld"*, *Rietveld Redux* (p. 55) is about Rietveld's original concept as much as Bennett's ideas.

GKB: The curves are mine!

SC: And the beads on the back.

GKB: They're great, aren't they? The chair is very comfortable. It's open on two sides, and you can move around in it. The beads obviously are not structural: they're a curtain! They're a visual back to the chair, so that you can get your backbone out.

SC: The beads move, they are action.

GKB: They sound good too. They tinkle. And I want you to notice, the beads are monochromatic. I could have painted them in wild colors.

SC: It seems you instead pursued a more unified tone.

GKB: Exactly.

SC: With curves and movement, *Rietveld Redux* has a sensual appeal.

GKB: Yeah, what Rietveld's chairs are about is his "less is more" sort of attitude, and I say "yeah, less is more, but I'll add a little and maybe it'll be a little bit more human."

SC: Why are you making chairs again now, whether they are of your design or inspired by other designs?

GKB: I started with the Rietvelds. I just needed to make something small, and, you know, it takes a week. You look at my older work, the big stuff, chests, desks, tables, cabinets, they could weight as much as 325 pounds, and I could throw that stuff around all by myself. Now I can't, I just don't…my hands hurt, I can't throw big stuff around; the chairs I can.

SC: How would you describe a good chair?

GKB: I had a woman tell me at UC Berkeley, "Garry, a chair's like a shoe." I said, "Really?" And she said, "Yeah, it's gotta be: light, strong, comfortable, and aesthetically pleasing." If you think about a chair and a shoe, they both meet those criteria. It's brilliant, I think, because they're both used heavily. A chair and a shoe take a lot of abuse.

Gerrit Rietveld (1888–1964)
Steltman Chair, 1963
27 1/2 x 19 3/4 x 17 3/4"
ARS/Vitra Design Museum

SC: Where do you start building a chair? The seat, the legs…is there a hierarchy in your way of building the structure of a chair?

GKB: If it's a laid-up chair, I start with the profile. And then I just fill it in. It's real simple. In *Sylvia's Chair* (p. 39), I definitely started from the seat, because I needed the seat to start it. And then once I got the seat, and it's got a slight tapered back to it, then I could start figuring out all the other parts. I would probably put the seat up on some blocks of wood or something, and look at it. I'd say, "Okay, well, let's do this." It's a very articulated and animated chair.

SC: Did you bend the wood?

GKB: The bentwood pieces came from Timothy Hoolsema, a steam-bender guy. He just bends stuff and when something cracks, or it's not right, they throw it in the pile, and I just asked for some of the pile. *Chair-881* (p. 41), *Chair-885* (p. 44), *Chair-900* (p. 40), to mention a few, *Scroll Chair* (p. 51) and some of the *Prototypes*, all use his bent wood.

SC: It seems to me, then, that one of your chairs may either start from woods and shapes available in your studio, or instead from a specific design in mind.

GKB: Well, with the bent pieces of wood, definitely, the material stimulated the ideas. But if I'm running one in my head that I want to make, then I'll have to find the material to fit the project.

SC: And how much do you rework your idea along the process?

GKB: I don't rework, I stick with what I start with most of the time. However, I repaint a lot when I'm using color. But when I was younger, I'd just go for it. And that's how I got so much work done. "Whoop! That was wrong, but we got that much work in, let's just finish it. On the next one I'll get that right." I'm working slower now because I'm thinking more. I don't want to waste something.

SC: Let's talk about how design and comfort come into play in your chairs and influence each other. Are these elements of some concern for you?

GKB: Some chairs are for looks and some I'm trying to design for comfort. Purposely comfortable. If they're for looks, I don't worry whether they're comfortable or not. I think I'm trying to make a chair for every man, so to speak. I'm not the kind of guy who will analyze why a chair is comfortable and why it's not, and try to work from that. I don't care about that. And if somebody sees something good in these chairs, measure it up, figure out why it works, and then run with it.

SC: You mean, taking-off your own designs?

GKB: I don't care. There's no way I can protect it anyway.

SC: Which brings us back, Garry, to those architects and designers whose work has been of inspiration for your take-offs in the series of chairs: Gerrit Rietveld, Charles Rennie Mackintosh, Frank Lloyd Wright, William Morris, Michael Thonet, Philippe Starck, even Martha Stewart! Let's talk about Frank Lloyd Wright: do you like his furniture?

GKB: No!

SC: Why?

GKB (talking loud in the microphone): Neither one of us does! Stefano doesn't like it either! Nobody should like it!

His architecture is sublime, not sublime, but it's awfully good. He was truly an innovator. But, again, back to architect's furniture design. We could look at his furniture and

Gord Peteran
Table Made of Wood, 2004.
Wood, 33" x 39" x 18 1/2".
Collection of Garry and Sylvia Bennett
Image © San Francisco Museum of Craft + Design

have some good laughs. I mean some of that stuff is ego that's going astray. You know one of the things that he said? When you're sworn in, "What is your profession?" "The world's greatest architect." One of the attorneys asked, "Why did you say you were the world's greatest architect?" "Because I was under oath." That's ego.

SC: In *Wiggle Wright* (p. 8), Frank Lloyd Wright is wiggling in your hands.

GKB: I was always going to make a Frank Lloyd Wrong, too.

SC: The hexagonal back is the reference to Wright's architecture, for his houses often feature floor plans with hexagonal designs, as does the furniture he designed for those houses.

GKB: Right. This chair, the mohair is forest green. The back is painted green and I knew I was going to gold leaf that back. Green, real rich green works better with gold. It's an amazing metal: when they make gold leaf, they can pound it so thin that when you hold a sheet of it up to light, it's only like a couple atoms thick, and the light that comes through is green. That's why the Arabs used gold and green.

SC: Did you start with the back for this chair? It's the visual gravity point of the chair…

GKB: No, I started with seat and the wiggles. That back was really hard to do. It's very strong too, and it's also a classic Frank Lloyd Wright chair insofar as it's brutally uncomfortable: you're straight up and down, like a church pew. So, that's how I really captured Wright, by making it uncomfortable. He works in all this rectilinear stuff, so I threw those wiggles in.

SC: Some of the chairs are inspired not by architects, but by studio furnituremakers. In particular, their visual and technical solutions have caught your attention. For example *#1 Gord* (p. 61), and *#2 Gord, Mark, Gupta* (p. 63), pay homage to Gord Peteran.

GKB: See Stefano, I work a little outside of the studio furniture idiom. And I've liked that it's been very good; as I'm sure you probably read somewhere, I was introduced at Berea College, Kentucky, as the Hunter S. Thompson of furnituremaking, which I really love. I just think that is mar-velous. But I think this guy, Gord, is gonna be *the* guy. I really do. Because he's really a conceptual artist. He makes furniture because he knows. I make it because I have to. I mean, I'm not gonna try to make art, but Gord just uses furniture, mainly as metaphor, in most of what he does. So that demi-lune table of his that Sylvia and I own—that's a brilliant piece of work. It got published in *Woodworking* magazine and, Jesus, the letters that John Levine got from these guys that make, you know, period furniture: "What do you print that shit in your magazine for?" That's the reaction I always liked and that's the reaction I know Gord likes. So this is an homage to Gord, basically. When I received that demi-lune I set right out to make this. *#1 Gord* chair is a little more structured than his work.

SC: Where do the scraps come from?

GKB: All out of my scrap bin and pieces of wood.

SC: It looks like there's a rolling pin.

GKB: Yeah, that's Mark Sfirri's.

SC: Oh, he turned it. So it is not all scraps?

GKB: No, it's an off-center rolling pin. Gord's a little more honest than me, he just goes with it. I manipulated the piece a little bit, the saw cuts here and there, but most of the scrap wood is just found. It's a really solid and yet comfortable chair: your back can lean back and your elbows can rest.

SC: Again, the color tones are carefully considered.

GKB: Yeah. This one being parts, there's all sorts of values to it. But it's a unified tone. The piece is unfinished, and I hope somebody who has it spills a glass of red wine on it, Just got finished working on his car, gets this armrest all nice and greasy and black. It'd be terrific with time.

SC: Tell me about your two versions of George Nakashima's *Conoid Chair* (p. 13), the "modified" and the "modernized." *Modified Nakashima* (p. 59) resembles more closely the *Conoid Chair*.

GKB: The *Conoid Chair* is just an ugly chair. But it's a beautifully engineered piece of work. Humor's a big part of these pieces. And my humor, I don't think is mocking. I think it's honest humor. See, if you look at someone's work and you just see either they're "Oh it's so precious" or "I'm so serious," well, now you're mine, okay? Now, the *Conoid Chair*: it's just not that hot. *Modified Nakashima* (p. 59) is as close as I could get to the *Conoid Chair* without having measured one. No! I actually measured it out of a picture. I threw a lot of curves in it!

SC: You measured it out of a picture.

GKB: I don't know as I've ever seen a real one. Well, I'm sure I have somewhere.

I just put a bunch of curves in, and he was terrified of a real freewheeling curve. I'm sure he got constipated if he ever thought of a freewheeling curve. I mean…

SC: *Modernized Nakashima* has lost completely the hand-crafted feeling. It looks so machine-made and mass-produced.

GKB: But you gotta admit that's a beautiful chair, an elegant chair. This chair would lend itself so well to mass-production.

SC: There are some significant structural changes in both of these chairs when compared to the original *Conoid Chair*.

GKB: Yeah, in the original the foot is outboard instead of inboard of the vertical, which makes it look kind of like a pigeon, or like it walks funny. It gives visual weight and sets it up in a very tenuous way to my eye. However, I was making humor of the design and then, I think, I must admire the chair, or I wouldn't have made what I figured was an improved version. It's somewhere in the recesses of my brain or scrotum or something. I probably do admire it. And I've always said I admire the engineering. So, don't stab me, George!

SC: Let's talk about your *Prototype* series; I know you are very excited about these chairs. *Red Chair* (frontispiece), *Joe's Chair* (p. 36), *Prototype series #1* (p. 36), and *Prototype series #3* (p. 37) mark a departure from the homage to—and appropriation of—the work of other designers.

GKB: They came so easy. So quickly, it just flowed. The only thing I know I was just rockin' and rollin,' man. These chairs took no more than two, maybe, three days max! These are just ideas; they're pure ideas. They're all painted white, with just prime paint, not a hard-finish enamel, and the seats are just canvas duck, except for the seat of *Yellow Chair*, that's painted. What's gonna happen, these chairs are going to get dirty.

SC: They'll take a patina.

GKB: Absolutely. It will look great. And you'll notice also that the edges of the legs are all sanded. In some chairs, it cuts back down to the wood. So you don't get a piece of wood that's all painted perfect. You have instead this nice line quality.

SC: You are outlining the chair!

GKB: Like a drawing. And it does. It comes out as a drawing.

SC: A three-dimensional drawing! This leads the conversation to another piece you made that you called *Chair Drawing With 2 Cushions* (p. 66). Rather than a chair, a *chair drawing*. Could you tell me more about this piece?

GKB: It's a plastic lawn chair. These chairs are so white and so pristine, I just drilled holes in it, tied steel tie wire around it, and it was quite laborious, and I said, "Well, I want it rusted." So I put it outside for about six months in the wintertime and it all rusted up and it's got nice staining and then I said, "Okay that's pretty good, but, you know, I could cast concrete cushions in here." These are concrete-cast cushions and the beauty of it is, when I cast the concrete on it, it just enveloped the tie wires, so it's almost its own rebar inside. I took a big, felt-tipped magic marker, and there's something in there that is ugly and it's really good. Ugly in that you can't cover it—it would take a lot of paint or you could grind it off. I drew these raindrops on it, and when that dried, I painted a couple coats back over it of Zinsser shellac, and in time, that marker comes through. So it's a very subtle sort of graphics. It's not like on the surface, it's down. I really like this chair.

SC: Well it looks to me like you pushed farther your idea of making a piece of furniture actually become –

GKB: A piece of sculpture. Trying to play artist, art guy. And I feel every now and then I can make a piece of art, but I don't try. I never try. This is probably my favorite piece in all these chairs, and I can't tell you why.

SC: The plastic chair was a clever solution. What else could have provided you with such a neutral blankness? The plastic chair is the white sheet of paper!

GKB: That's right. It would've been really pretentious of me to make a chair and then just tie wire around it. Why bother? Get a nice white chair. And with the rusted steel, Jesus, you're in business!

SC: A white plastic lawn chair also served as the base for another piece, the *Martha Stewart Chair* (p. 67).

GKB: Well, it starts with the big ties that hold the cushion on the back. That's a stroke of genius! I mean, I could've hung those cushions on there easier. But, no, you gotta have those big bows, you know?

SC: And a very nice garden patio-like design for the cushion.

GKB: I was initially thinking of gingham, the little pink and red and white square gingham. And I said, "No," and I came across this upholstery and I said, "That's it!" Because it's subdued, kind of, and it's gucky as hell and it's really outdoor stuff. So, this chair started out *Martha Stewart*. I just wanted to make it. I said, "Well, I'm gonna do how the housewife can, in her spare time, fix up some of her lawn chairs." No way could they do this…

SC: You mean covering the arms with wood…

GKB: Yes, it's beautiful oak, white oak. It's goddamned near perfect, and it was so hard to make. Because it's 8th-inch strips of oak heated in hot water so I could bend them and then I could only bend one at a time, because the plastic doesn't have enough resistance. So the first one I bent, and then when that one dried—and this took forever, because you have to wait for the wood to dry—I could pretty easily bend the second one into it. Then I had enough structure that I clamped and glued it. And at that point, I'm doing both sides, and it gets pretty strong, so I could use the wood strip itself as its own form to mold the next series. I think there are six layers of 8th-inch oak in there. And it's all screwed very cleanly in the back. You can barely see it. It's screwed to the plastic. You look at these two chairs, *Chair Drawing* and *Martha Stewart,* and there's a nice continuity there, although they're totally different in look.

SC: You are using the same medium, the plastic lawn chair, but with different meanings or rather purposes: in *Chair Drawing With 2 Cushions*, the plastic chair is the mere and almost invisible base, a white background to draw on. In the *Martha Stewart Chair,* on the contrary, the plastic chair affirms its presence while stressing its affordable *and* cheap-looking qualities.

GKB: I hope she buys it. She probably doesn't have that aesthetic. It'd be kind of neat though if she did buy it. And then she would have elevated herself because she appreciated my work. No, just kidding.

SC: There is a chair produced since the 1870s, a chair one could consider a predecessor of the plastic lawn chair, thinking of its wide diffusion in café patios, that prompted a totally new direction in the chair series. The Thonet *Vienna Café Chair* was used as readymade in your *Thonet Wall series* (pp. 70-75). Earlier in the series, however, you made a floor piece, titled *Thonet* (p. 16).

GKB: Yeah, the armrests were really hard to make, because I had to make a right and a left. They're fairly strong because they're steel armature inside and there's a lot of fiberglass and stuff. They're pretty strong, but they're not quite matched up. One's a little off and I didn't want to try to do it any better.

SC: They resemble horns…

GKB: Scrotums! Well, I don't know. This chair model is so formal, and I also wanted something that looked very sensual coming off of that, something really organic. Let's get wings, glue feathers on ourselves, get on top of the barn, and jump off and see if we can fly. Okay? That is pretty much my philosophy. It really is. But look at the color. Those colors are very subtle: ocher, yellow, and then these are titty pinks.

SC: I like the green in the back.

GKC: Yeah, that's just a really nice sort of brown-green. Let me see… yes it is! This is, I'll tell you man, if I had Frank Stella's ability to put color on something, I'd be the greatest furnituremaker of our time. That's how I feel. You know, Stella can put those olive drab greens and pinks and stuff together, but I just don't have that control. I don't have that knowledge. And these are definitely his greens, I definitely had him in mind.

SC: Your *Thonet Wall Series* chairs mark a totally new direction.

GKB: I wanted to take the chairs off the floor and put them on the wall. I am getting really tired of Garry Knox Bennett the furnituremaker, you know? I've got a good reputation, but, boy, I just know that I got a little extra in me. That's why I like these wall pieces, whether they're good or not. I like them, because now I'm kind of free of this floor thing.

SC: You had already cut a chair in two in the past. Before the *African* chairs, your first chair was an Eames *LCW Chair* that you sliced in two.

GKB: Yeah. The reason I cut it in two is when I looked at it I liked the shape of the half. It's quite a beautiful shape in profile. It was a very elaborate way to cut it in half, but I did it, and then I mounted it with a piece of aluminum with Formica ColorCore® on either side. White on one side, black on the other. The white side had the black painted chair, the black side had the white painted chair. But it was only done because I like the shape of it. So it's only aesthetics.

SC: Why did you chose Thonet's *Vienna Café Chair* for this wall series and not another chair?

GKB: Because I had them, and I love the line quality. I had one kicking around the studio for years, it got paint and stuff all over it. I mean, I would put stuff on it and paint it. And one day I looked at that and I said "Well…" And I sawed it, and I made a jig. I've got a hand saw, a big beautiful hand saw. And I could saw that just perfect, where I wanted. And it's not sawed in half; it's sawed at an angle. So, that was the first one. It was *Chair #908* (p. 75). It's the one that started *all* the others.

SC: You already had in mind to draw and paint the shadows when you mounted the chair on the back panel?

GKB: Yeah. I brought it up from the shop and leaned it against the wall; I have some hard light here and I mounted it one night and traced these shadows with a pencil. Here's the problem, and I think Matthew Kangas addressed it: the first one or two pieces in a series I do are generally the best, because I always figure out a way to do it a little better next time. And that's the kiss of death. The best part is

Split Eames Chair, 1984
Eames LCW Chair, aluminum, Formica ColorCore®, paint, 36" x 24" x 24"
Collection of James and Joanne Rapp.
Photograph © George Erml

the fresh part, the first idea. I like the first ones because they are honest. I forgot to draw the shadows in some points. I got so carried away that I forgot it. The attention to the line totally is all over my work. I mean, again, my work is not in the round, so to speak, and yet it is three-dimensional. Somehow, man, I just really decided I want to pursue this line quality. And I'll spend an inordinate amount of time when I'm drawing a curve on a piece of wood to make part of a chair or a table or something. There will be a lot of erasing and a lot of times what I'll do is I'll paint the wood white so that I can really see, you know. And I spend a lot of time with that curve.

SC: That line is more important than the volumes…

GKB: The line—if the line's good—it's gonna take care of the rest of the piece. It's symbiotic.

SC: Even when you have very chubby volumes, like chairs as in *Stubby Stark* (p. 52), you still have the line in the back enticing the eye.

GKB: Yes, absolutely. The chair itself is dumb. That particular aluminum line supporting the back sets that chair. I mean that really sets that chair. And it's a gorgeous goddamn line.

SC: The idea to put a chair on the wall is not new.

GKB: No it's not. Shakers hung their chairs on the wall. They seem to have a sensitivity to just a very simple design, sure, that was their trip.

SC: When do you think ideas for the chair series will run dry?

GKB: Oh, it's dry here. It's dry here.

SC: Are you focusing only on the wall pieces at the moment?

GKB: Right. I want to treat these things more conceptually. But I will still keep making chairs because I like it. And I will concentrate on making—I hope—a simple chair that is back to that comfort, strength, and lightness concepts we discussed. Something that is like one of the great commercial chairs around.

Do you ever watch "Antiques Roadshow"?

SC: No.

GKB: I don't like antiques, but I watch that show religiously. My point is the people who want antique furniture want that age on it, they want that patina. And that patina of time is so beautiful for me. You know? Every once in a while somebody phones me and says, "Oh we've got this ding, this crack." Well, leave it. These people are really anal about work that they own. You know, they're new collectors. I'm sure the same thing happened in the 1700s when the maid scratched the new piece. So in my lifetime I can make that choice. I don't want to see the fucking thing again. I don't have the time to refinish, especially with some of the techniques I used. I've got work to do, I don't need to revisit, you know? I had a person phone me up, from Maryland or Delaware or New Jersey, somewhere out there. He said, "We have a piece of yours. We really like it. It's a coffee table." And I said, "What's it like?" He described it and I said, "Oh, yeah, I know the table. That's a good one." Well, I built coffee tables and I would put a shelf underneath so you could put books or magazines on it. And had cut down a tree in the backyard, and I made these real thin planks and they were the trays, the bottom part of this thing. And he said, "Well, one of the planks split." And I said, "Well, that happens with wood." And he said, "We're really concerned about the crack." And I said, "Please, don't worry about the crack. It'll be all right." And he says, "Well, you know, we'd like to do something about it. Maybe we'll send it to you." And I said to myself, "Yeah, okay, they're not going to send it. A big fucking thing like that." And one day the bell rings and there's this fucking truck out there. It's a big fucking crate. They pull the crate out and I'm, "What the hell is this?" The driver says, "Are you Garry Bennett?" "Yeah." "This is 130 4th?" "Yeah." "Sign here." I took the thing apart and there's the coffee table. Took it out of the crate and looked and sure enough there's one of these planks, a little thin, it's got a crack in it. I took the table, turned it upside down on the sawhorses, got a felt-tipped pen, wrote "This crack okay," drew an arrow to it, signed it GKB, put it back in the crate, phoned the trucking company, never heard back from the guy. "This crack okay."

SC: You signed the same piece twice: once when you originally made it and again when you repaired it!

GKB: I know, I know! I loved it when I did it.

SC: Garry Knows Best!

GKB: Turn that tape recorder off, let's just enjoy ourselves…

Oakland, California, April 4–5, 2006

Stefano Catalani
Curator
Bellevue Arts Museum

EXHIBITION HISTORY

Born: Alameda, California 1934

Attended: California College of the Arts (formerly CCAC) Oakland, California

SELECTED SOLO EXHIBITIONS

2005

Garry Knox Bennett: Preoccupations of a Serial Chairmaker, Oakland Museum of California at City Center, Gallery 555 and Sculpture Court, Oakland, CA, January 20–March 25, 2005.

2004

Garry Knox Bennett, Leo Kaplan Modern, New York, December 4, 2003–January 17, 2004.

2002

Garry Knox Bennett "Reconstructed Twirlings," Leo Kaplan Modern, New York, October17–November 9, 2002.

2001

Made in Oakland: The Furniture of Garry Knox Bennett, 30 year Retrospective, Opened at the American Craft Museum, NY, traveled to Oakland Museum of California.

Garry Knox Bennett, Leo Kaplan Modern, New York, January 20–February 24, 2001.

Garry Knox Bennett, Tercera Gallery, San Francisco CA

What's In a Name? New Jewelry by Garry Knox Bennett a.k.a. Gerraldo Bennucci, CA Julie: Artisans' Gallery, New York.

1999

Garry Knox Bennett, Leo Kaplan Modern, New York, May 7–29, 1999.

1996

Garry Knox Bennett, 100 Lamps, Peter Joseph Gallery, New York, December 4, 1996–January 18, 1997.

1994

Garry Knox Bennett, Peter Joseph Gallery, New York, September 22–October 22, 1994.

1992

Furniture: West Coast Survey of Large and Small Works by Garry Knox Bennett, North Light Gallery (now Stewart-Kummer Gallery), Gualala, California, September 5–October 15, 1992.

1990

Garry Knox Bennett, Furniture as Sculpture, The Hand and the Spirit Gallery, Scottsdale, Arizona, January 2–31, 1990.

1989

Garry Knox Bennett, New Works in Bronze, Brendan Walter Gallery, Santa Monica, California, January 12–February 18, 1989.

Garry Knox Bennett: New Furniture, Snyderman Gallery, Philadelphia, May 7–June 30, 1989.

1987

Garry Knox Bennett: Furniture Maker, Snyderman Gallery, Philadelphia, May 3–June 21,1987.

Wendell Castle, Garry Knox Bennett, Fred Baier, Alexander F. Milliken Gallery, New York, September 12–October 14, 1987 (3-person show).

1986

Garry Knox Bennett, Elaine Potter Gallery, San Francisco, January 21–February 22, 1986.

1984

Garry Knox Bennett: Furniture Maker, Snyderman Gallery, Philadelphia, May 6–July 1, 1984.

1983

Garry Bennett: Benches and Other Fantasy Furniture, The Hand and the Spirit Gallery, Scottsdale, Arizona, January 13–February 7, 1983.

Garry Bennett: Sculptural Furniture, Foster Goldstrom Fine Arts, San Francisco, September 15–October 22, 1983.

1980

Works by Garry Knox Bennett, Workbench Gallery, New York, September 10–October 19,1980.

1977

Garry Bennett: Clocks, Julie: Artisans' Gallery, New York, February 1977.

1973

Garry Bennett: Clocks, Lights, Jewelry, The Egg and the Eye, (subsequently The Craft and Folk Art Museum) Los Angeles, July 24–August 21, 1973.

SELECTED GROUP EXHIBITIONS

2005

Under Cover: Upholstery in Contemporary Furniture, Gallery NAGA, Boston, MA, November 11–December 17, 2005.

Turning Around the World. Wood Turning Center, Philadelphia, PA, November 4, 2005–January 7, 2006.

2003

Corporal Identity – Body Language, 9th Triennial, Museum of Arts & Design, New York; the Museum für Angewandte Kunst, Frankfurt, Germany; the Klingspor-Museum, Offenbach, Germany, 2003.

20th Anniversary Exhibition: A Celebration of Work by Artists Exhibited Over the Last 20 Years, Snyderman Gallery, Philadelphia, PA, May 2–June 28, 2003.

Turned Multiples III, Wood Turning Center, Philadelphia, PA, March 7–April 26, 2003.

The Maker's Hand: American Studio Furniture 1940-1990, Museum of Fine Arts, Boston, MA, November 12, 2003–February 8, 2004.

2002

Materials & Contemporary Illusions: Innovations in Lathe Turning, The Lynn Tendler Bignell Gallery, Brookfield, CT, August 25–October 13, 2002.

The Right Stuff: a juried exhibition of Upholstered Furniture, Humanities Gallery, University of Wisconsin-Madison, May 31–June 14, 2002. Exhibition traveled to three additional venues.

2001

25 Years of Fine Craftsmanship: Brookfield Craft Center Faculty 1976–2000, The Lynn Tendler Bignell Gallery & The Silo Gallery, Brookfield, CT, June 10–July 29, 2001.

1999

The Art of Craft: Works from the Saxe Collection, Fine Arts Museum of San Francisco, June 26–October 17, 1999.

Material Witness: Masters from California Crafts, Crocker Museum, Sacramento, California, October 29, 1999–January 2, 2000.

1997

Hello Again!: A New Wave of Recycled Art and Design, Oakland Museum of California, February 15–July 27, 1997.

1996

Hot Rods and Customs: The Men and Machines of "California's Car Culture," Oakland Museum of California, August 12–October 19, 1996

1995

Museum for a New Century, Craft and Folk Art Museum, Los Angeles, May 13–December 31, 1995.

1994

Masterworks II, Peter Joseph Gallery, New York, January 20–February 26, 1994.

1991

A California Complement: Recent Studio Furniture from the Bay Area, Oakland Museum of California (in conjunction with *New American Furniture: The Second Generation of Studio Furniture makers*), Oakland, California, February 9–April 21, 1991.

American Crafts: The Nation's Collection, Renwick Gallery of the Smithsonian American Art Museum, Washington, D.C., April 1991.

Explorations II: The New Furniture, The American Craft Museum, New York, May 9–August 4, 1991.

1990

Oakland Artists '90, Oakland Museum of California, March 24–July 1, 1990.

Art for Everyday, Snyderman Gallery, Philadelphia, September 2–October 7, 1990.

1989

New American Furniture: The Second Generation of Studio Furniture makers. Museum of Fine Arts, Boston, December 8, 1989-March 18, 1990. Traveled to Renwick Gallery of the Smithsonian American Art Museum, Washington, D.C., April 20-September 3, 1990; The Contemporary Arts Center, Cincinnati, Ohio, November 9, 1990-January 8, 1991; Oakland Museum of California, Oakland, California, February 9-April 21, 1991.

Contemporary Furniture from San Francisco and Boston, Gallery NAGA, Boston, March 30–April 29, 1989.

Craft Today USA, The American Craft Museum, New York, 1989. Exhibition traveled extensively out of the country for 3 1/2 years: Musée des Arts Décoratifs, Paris; Museum of Applied Art, Helsinki; Museum für Kunsthandwerk, Frankfurt, 1989-1990; Zacheta Gallery, Warsaw; Musée des Arts Décoratifs, Lausanne; Museum of Decorative Applied & Folk Art, Moscow; State Painting & Sculpture Museum, Ankara. 1991; The Oslo Museum of Applied Art, Oslo; St. Peter's Abbey, Ghent; Amerika Haus, Berlin; The Zappeion, Athens, 1992; Slovak National Gallery, Bratislava, Czechoslovakia; The Grassi Museum, Leipzig; Sala Sant Jaume de la Fundacio "La Caixa", Barcelona; The Gulbenkian, Lisbon, 1993.

Innovations in Wood, The Society for Art in Crafts, Pittsburgh, Pennsylvania, November 16, 1989–January 7, 1990.

Contemporary Furniture: 13 Major Figures, Gallery NAGA, Boston, December 7–22, 1989.

1988

California Furnishings: A Statewide Survey of Progressive Design, Monterey Peninsula Museum of Art, California, December 12, 1987–February 28, 1988.

1986

Fine Wood, Euphrat Gallery, De Anza College, Cupertino, California, March 25–May 8, 1986.

Craft Today: Poetry of the Physical, American Craft Museum, New York, October 26, 1986–March 22, 1987. Exhibition traveled to five additional venues.

1985

Material Evidence: New Color Techniques in Handmade Furniture, (opened at Workbench Gallery, New York, April 11–May 27, 1984, under the title *Material Evidence: Master Craftsmen Explore ColorCore*), circulated by Smithsonian Traveling Exhibition Service to the Renwick Gallery of the Smithsonian American Art Museum, Washington, D.C., April 7–September 22,1985.

Contemporary American Woodworkers, Snyderman Gallery, Philadelphia, December 8, 1985–January 19, 1986.

1981

Alumni Show, California College of Arts and Crafts, Oakland, California, 1981.

Craft and Folk Art Museum (formerly the Egg and the Eye), Los Angeles, 1981.

Elements Gallery, New York, 1981.

1980

California Woodworking, Oakland Museum of California, Oakland, California, December 16, 1980–February 15, 1981.

1979

New Handmade Furniture: American Furniture Makers Working in Hard Wood, Museum of Contemporary Crafts (now American Craft Museum), New York, May 5–July 15, 1979. Exhibition traveled to ten venues.

1977

Bay Area Artists Exhibition, Oakland Museum of California, Oakland, California, June 11–19, 1977.

1975

Bay Area Artists Exhibition, Oakland Museum of California, August 22–28, 1975.

1974

Euphrat Gallery, De Anza College, Cupertino, California, 1974 (Garry Knox Bennett Electroprint; Purchase Award).

1971

Metal Experience, Oakland Museum of California, June 5–July 4, 1971.

1961

Sculpture Annual, San Francisco Museum of Art, spring 1961 (award).

1960

79th Annual Painting and Sculpture Exhibition of the San Francisco Art Association, San Francisco Museum of Art, March 24–April 24, 1960.

SELECTED BIBLIOGRAPHY

EXHIBITION CATALOGS

Contemporary Studio Case Furniture: The Inside Story. Madison: Elvehjem Museum of Art, University of Wisconsin, 2002.

Cooke, Edward S., Jr. *New American Furniture: The Second Generation of Studio Furnituremakers.* Boston: Museum of Fine Arts, 1989.

Corporal Identity- Body Language: 9th Triennial for Form and Content – USA and Germany. New York and Frankfurt: Museum of Arts & Design, New York; Museum of Applied Arts, Frankfurt; Klingspor-Museum, Offenbach, 2004

Craft Today USA. New York: American Craft Museum, 1989.

Curv-iture: Studio Furniture Celebrates the Curve. Interview with juror Garry Knox Bennett conducted by Andrew H. Glasgow. Savannah, GA; Hickory, NC; Raleigh, NC: organized by The Furniture Society, Asheville, NC, 2004-2005.

Dovetailing Art and Life: the Bennett Collection. San Francisco: San Francisco Museum of Craft + Design, 2004.

Dunnigan, John. "Under Cover: Some Thoughts On Upholstered Furniture." Booklet presented for *Under Cover: Upholstery in Contemporary Furniture.* Boston: Gallery NAGA, 2005.

Ilse-Neuman, Ursula. *Explorations II: The New Furniture.* New York: American Craft Museum.1991.

The Maker's Hand: American Studio Furniture 1940–1990. Boston: Museum of Fine Arts, 2003–2004.

Material evidence: New Color Techniques in Handmade Furniture. Washington D.C.: Smithsonian Institution Traveling Exhibition Service, 1985.

Scents of Purpose: Artists Interpret the Spice Box. San Francisco: The Contemporary Jewish Museum, 2005.

Smith, Paul J., and Edward Lucie-Smith. *Craft Today: Poetry of the Physical.* New York: American Craft Museum, 1986.

BOOKS

Beckerdite, Luke. *American Furniture.* Milwaukee: The Chipstone Foundation, 2002.

Bennett, Gary Knox et al., *Made in Oakland: The Furniture of Garry Knox Bennett.* New York: American Craft Museum (now Museum of Arts & Design), 2001.

Conway, Patricia. *Art for Everyday: The New Craft Movement.* New York: Clarkson Potter Publishers, 1990.

Fitzgerald, Oscar P. *Four Centuries of American Furniture: An Updated, Expanded Version of the Classic Three Centuries of American Furniture, the Standard Reference to Antique, Collectible, and Museum Furniture.* Iola, WI: Krause Publications, 1995.

Hosaluk, Michael. *Scratching the Surface: Art and Content in Contemporary Wood.* Madison: GUILD Publishing, 2002.

Kelsey, John. *Furniture Studio 3: Furniture Makers Exploring Digital Technologies.* Asheville, NC: The Furniture Society, 2005.

Meilach, Dona Z. *Art Jewelry Today.* Atglen, PA: Schiffer Publishing Ltd., 2003.

Pearson, Katherine. *American Craft: A Source Book for the Home.* New York: Stewart Tabori & Chang, 1993.

Princenthal, Nancy. *A Creative Legacy: A History of the National Endowment for the Arts Visual Artists' Fellowship Program 1966-1995.* Introduction by William Ivey; essay by Nancy Princenthal; essay by Jennifer Dowley. New York: Harry N. Abrams Inc., 2001.

Stone, Michael A. *Contemporary American Woodworkers.* Layton, Utah: Gribbs M. Smith, 1986.

ARTICLES

Adamson, Glenn. "A Writer's Block." *Woodwork,* no. 80 (April 2003).

Beeler, Monique. "He put fun in furniture: Knox Bennett just your average unclassifiable blue-collar functional artisan." *The San Mateo County Times,* July 17, 2001.

———. "Crafting Art: its not all macramé: Tin cans, scrap wood count in new Museum." *The Oakland Tribune,* October 28, 2004.

Binzen, Jonathan. "Spectacular! Stirring! Fun! A longtime skeptic experiences a (partial) conversion." *Woodwork,* no. 71 (October 2001).

Caldwell, Brian. " 'Preoccupations of a Serial Chairmaker' in Oakland." *Woodshop News,* vol. XIX, no. 4 (March 2005).

———. "The Amazing Mr. Bennett." *Woodshop News,* vol. XX, no. 2 (January 2006).

Craddick, Hannah. "Bennett's work goes Against the Grain." *Alameda magazine,* volume 1, issue 2 (Nov/Dec 2002).

Goldman, Pam. "Profile: Garry Knox Bennett." *Woodworker West,* vol. 14, no. 4 (July/Aug 2001).

Hanna, Kathleen and Karin Nelson. "From Hand to Hand: Masters as Mentors." *A Report,* vol. 18, no. 3, 2002. From the Museum of Craft & Folk Art, San Francisco.

Kelsey, John. "How To Be Garry Knox Bennett: the bad boy of Oakland continues to surprise, annoy, and delight." *Woodwork,* no.71 (October 2001).

Kilduff, Paul. "The School of Hard Knox." *The East Bay Monthly,* vol.35, no.1 (October 2004).

Kirwin, Liza, and Joan Lord. "A Toolkit of Dreams: Conversations with American Craft Artists." *Smithsonian Archives of American Art Journal,* vol. 43, no.1-2 (2004).

Lavine, John. "What's in a Name?" *Woodwork,* no.91 (February 2005).

———. "Leftovers." *Woodwork,* no.79 (February 2003).

Martin, Terry. "A Treasure Trove of Wood Art." *Turning Points,* volume 18, no. 1 (Fall 2005).

———. "Materials & Contemporary Illusions: Innovations in Lathe Turning." *Turning Points*, volume 15, no. 4 (Winter 2003).

Metcalf, Bruce. "American Studio Furniture 1940-1990." *American Craft*, volume 64, no. 1 (Feb/Mar 2004).

Stone, Michael A. "Garry Knox Bennett." *Woodwork*, no.71 (October 2001).

Wasserman, Abby. "The 3 Faces of Geraldo." *The Museum of California magazine*, volume 25, no. 2 (2001).

Weddington, Diane. "Bennett doesn't want to rest on his laurels." *The Oakland Tribune*, January 7, 2003.

White, Cheryl. "Garry Knox Bennett." *American Craft*, volume 61, no. 5 (Oct/Nov 2001).

Whitman, Marina. "The Right Stuff: a Dialogue between Furniture and Fiber." *FIBERARTS*, vol.30, no.3 (Nov/ Dec 2003).

VIDEO

Artist At Work: Garry Knox Bennett: Spark segment, 2005 KQED inc.

Cut Loose: New American Furniture Makers: San Francisco. Minott Weihnacht Productions, 1994 (1994 Cine Golden Eagle award).

Dialog & Interview at the Oakland Museum: Garry with John R. Marlowe and Abby Wasserman, 2001 retrospective exhibition, Oakland venue.

ARCHIVES

Smithsonian Institution, Archives of American Art, Nanette L. Laitman Documentation Project, 2003: All papers and personal files, photographs and a complete oral history (available on line). All material from ongoing career will continue to be archived.

HONORS & AWARDS

2004 Merit Award, Lifetime Achievement – Furniture Society
1996 American Craft Council, College of Fellows
1984 Merit Grant, National Endowment for the Arts
1975 Award, Contemporary Crafts of the Americas
1974 Award, De Anza College
1960 Award, San Francisco Museum of Modern Art

MUSEUM COLLECTIONS

Museum of Arts & Design, New York

De Young Museum, San Francisco

Fine Arts Museum, Mobile AL

Judah Magnus Museum, Oakland CA

Mint Museum of Craft + Design, Charlotte NC

Montreal Museum of Art, Canada

Museum of Fine Arts, Boston MA

Oakland Museum of California

Racine Art Museum, WI

Renwick Gallery Smithsonian American Art Museum, Washington, DC

San Francisco Museum of Modern Art, CA

Garry Knox Bennett

CHECKLIST OF THE EXHIBITION

Upholstered chair #1
2001
Powdercoat, steel chairs, plastic zip ties
35" x 20 1/2" x 24"

GR series #1: "New Ladderback"
2003
Maple, Douglas fir, nickel-plated brass, GKB fabricated ladder
41 3/4" x 14 5/8" x 22"

GR series #2: "Old Ladderback"
2003
Maple, cherry, bone, beads, copper
51 1/2" x 14 5/8" x 17 1/4"

GR series #3: "Duncan Rietveld"
2003
Dyed mahogany, lacewood, 23K gold-plated brass
39 5/8" x 14 3/4" x 17 1/2"

GR series #4: "Granny Rietveld"
2003
Red oak, hand-caned seat, polished brass
33 3/4" x 17" x 17 1/8"

GR series #5: "Chas Rietveld"
2003
Enameled wood, nickel-plated brass
54 1/2" x 15" x 17 1/8"

GR series #6: "Wing Chair"
2003
Lacewood, polished aluminum, lacquer
41 3/4" x 29 1/4" x 17"

GR series #7: "Windsor"
2003
Enameled wood, lacquered wood, upholstered leather, silver-plated brass
30" x 23 1/2" x 22 1/4"

GR series #8: "Great Granny Rietveld"
2003
Wood, upholstered cotton
30 3/4" x 15" x 18"

GR series #10 : "Chair-788"
2003
Lacquered wood, yellow satinwood
29 1/8" x 15 1/4" x 15 3/4"

GR series #12: "Chair-790"
2003
Cherry, polished brass
32" x 14 1/2" x 16 1/2"

GR series #14: "XYZ Chair"
2003
Lacquered wood, aluminum
33 1/2" x 15" x 18"

GR series #15: "Thong"
2003
Douglas fir, cherry, paint
34 1/2" x 18 3/4" x 17 1/4"

Prototype Series #3
2003
Painted wood, upholstered canvas duck, 23K gold-plated brass, stainless steel wire
29 1/2" x 18" x 22"

Prototype Series #4: "Joe's Chair"
2003
Painted wood, aluminum, upholstered canvas duck
21 1/2" x 21 1/2" x 22 1/2"

#1 Gord
2004
Mixed hardwood
51" x 25" x 24"

#2 Gord, Mark, Gupta
2004
Mixed exotic wood, carved Indian panel
45 1/2" x 24 1/2" x 27 1/2"

Chair Drawing With 2 Cushions
2004
Plastic chair, steel wire, cement, paint
34 1/2" x 22" x 24"

Chair-851
2004
Enameled wood, mahogany, lacquered G-10
32" x 26" x 26"

Chair-857
2004
Enameled wood, upholstered leather, G-10, 23K gold-plated brass
31 1/4" x 19 1/2" x 23 1/2"

Chair-858
2004
Lacquered wood, white oak, G-10, gouache, brass, pigmented epoxy
33 1/4" x 20 1/2" x 26"

Char
2004
California black walnut, Douglas fir, washboard, copper
38 3/4" x 15 1/4" x 16"

Granny Starck
2004
Yellow cedar, lacquered wood, aluminum, upholstered leather
31" x 16" x 32"

Little Maurice
2004
Mahogany, polished brass, upholstered faux alligator leather
38 1/2" x 27 1/2" x 30"

Martha Stewart Chair
2004
Plastic chair, lacquered white oak, cotton upholstery
35" x 22" x 25"

Modernized Nakashima
2004
Mahogany, polished brass
36 1/4" x 18 1/2" x 24"

Modified Nakashima
2004
Oregon walnut
35" x 19 1/4" x 23 1/2"

Prototype Series #1
2004
Shellacked wood, gouache, 23K gold-plated brass
32" x 20" x 20 1/2"

Prototype Series #2: "Red Chair"
2004
Painted wood, aluminum, upholstered canvas duck
30 3/4" x 20" x 27"

Rietveld Redux
2004
Painted wood, beads
33 1/4" x 24" x 20 1/4"

Stubby Starck
2004
Yellow cedar, aluminum, upholstered velvet
29" x 16" x 22"

Sylvia's Chair
2004
Lacquered wood, hand-caned seat
31" x 22" x 25"

Thonet
2004
Chair, fiberglass, enamel paint, hand-caned seat
34 1/2" x 25" x 17"

Wiggle Wright
2004
Mahogany, upholstered mohair, 23K gold leaf
36" x 22" x 16"

Chair-881
2005
Lacquered wood, figured maple, white oak, machine-caned seat, upholstered leather, brass
34 3/4" x 23 1/2" x 25"

Chair-883
2005
Maple, machine-caned seat, upholstered leather, gouache on plywood
35" x 23" x 28"

Chair-885
2005
Maple, upholstered cotton
28" x 20" x 26"

Chair-886
2005
Enameled wood, machine caned seat
31" x 18" x 24"

Chair-887
2005
Walnut, matte silver-plated copper, upholstered embossed leather, Formica ColorCore®
32 3/4" x 27 1/2" x 32"

Chair-895
2005
Walnut, maple, cherry
30" x 24 1/2" x 21"

Chair-912
2005
Wood, paint, upholstered embossed leather
31" x 22 1/2" x 25"

Chinese Platform Chair #2: Late Oaktown Dynasty; 1934–____.
2005
Lacquered wood, pigmented epoxy, bamboo, velvet upholstery
39" x 22 3/4" x 25 1/2"

Chinese Platform Chair #4: Late Oaktown Dynasty; 1934– ____.
2005
Rosewood, hand-caned seat, polished brass
43" x 25" x 26"

Chinese Platform Chair #5: Late Oaktown Dynasty; 1934- ____.
2005
Lacquered wood, PVC, 23K & 24K gold leaf, velvet upholstery
39" x 22" x 26"

Scroll Chair
2005
Dyed walnut, brass, wire, synthetic leather upholstery
37" x 25" x 32 1/2"

Chair-900
2006
23K Gold leafed wood, yellow satinwood, pigmented epoxy, upholstered velvet
26" x 21" x 24"

Chair-915
2006
Douglas fir, enameled wood
34" x 20" x 23"

Thonet wall Chair-908
2006
Chair, wood panel, paint
48" x 36" x 12 1/4"

Thonet wall series 1/4
2006
Chair, wood panel, paint
47 1/2" x 36 1/2" x 12 1/2"

Thonet wall series 2/4
2006
Chair, wood panel, paint
47 1/2" x 36 1/2" x 12 1/2"

Thonet wall series 3/4
2006
Chair, wood panel, paint
47 1/2" x 36 1/2" x 12 1/2"

Thonet wall series 4/4
2006
Chair, wood panel, paint
47 1/2" x 36 1/2" x 12 1/2"

ACKNOWLEDGMENTS

My sincere appreciation to Bellevue Arts Museum, its Board, staff, patrons, docents, guilds, and volunteers for their support for this exhibition of my most recent work.

Executive Director and Chief Curator Michael Monroe, who called me and said: "Do you want to have a chair show?" I said "yes!" He said: "It might be quicker than you think!" It was! Thank you, Michael!

Curator for this exhibition Stefano Catalani: Lavorare con te su questa mostra è stata una grande esperienza. Sei arrivato nel mio studio preparato a lavorare sodo, ben informato ed armato di una grande passione per le arti. In più ti piace mangiare! Cosa si potrebbe desiderare di più in un curatore!! For your thoroughness, expertise, and enthusiasm, thank you, Stefano!

My sincere appreciation to Glenn Adamson, Stefano Catalani, Arthur C. Danto, and Matthew Kangas for the informative essays each has contributed. Special thanks to Lorry Dudley and Edward S. Cooke, Jr., for their kindness and support always.

So many talented people contribute to an exhibition and I am truly indebted to all who have participated in this one. My thanks and gratitude to all and especially the following:

Gena Schwam, Registrar, for her skillful attention to detail, and to the entire staff at Bellevue Arts Museum, for their work on this exhibition.

Photographer M. Lee Fatherree, for documenting my work with immense skill and care.

Alison McLennan, for her "young eyes," work ethic, and skill.

For the skills I cannot count as my own: James Luque, Luques Upholstery; Roberto Lazo, Lazo's Caning; Timothy Hoolsema, Michigan Chair Company; and Scott Atthowe, Atthowe Fine Art Services.

To chair makers, past and present, who started me on this particular journey, thank you!

To my wife Sylvia, 46 years and running, I love you, completely.

Garry Knox Bennett

BELLEVUE ARTS MUSEUM BOARD OF TRUSTEES 2006

President: Angela Sutter

Board Members

Diane Babbitt
June Bartell
Keith Gormley Baldwin
Ron Bayley
Kimberly Becklund
Susan Edelheit
Richard Collette
Alexandra Muse Ehrlich
Alex Florence
George Grubb
John Frank
Mark Haley
Lawrence Hebner
Jerry Hendin
John Hepler
Mark Horiuchi
Anna Littlewood
Norma Klorfine
Larry Metcalf
Bill Monkman
Valerie Piha
Frank Statkus
Cappy Thompson
Susan Thurston

Peter Horvtiz (Emeritus)

Docent President: Cecelia Teddy
Guild Representative: Meredith Adami